A JUMBLE
OF THOUGHTS

JAMES SITTON

authorHOUSE®

AuthorHouse™
1663 Liberty Drive
Bloomington, IN 47403
www.authorhouse.com
Phone: 1-800-839-8640

Photo credit to James Sitton
Interior Illustrations by James Sitton

This book is a work of non-fiction. Unless otherwise noted, the author and the publisher make no explicit guarantees as to the accuracy of the information contained in this book and in some cases, names of people and places have been altered to protect their privacy.

Published by AuthorHouse 10/21/2014

ISBN: 978-1-4969-3137-5 (sc)
ISBN: 978-1-4969-3136-8 (hc)
ISBN: 978-1-4969-3135-1 (e)

Library of Congress Control Number: 2014913834

PREFACE

According to *Webster's New Riverside University Dictionary*, "preface" is defined as

> **1.a.** An introductory statement or essay, used, by the author, explaining the scope, intention, or background of a book: FOREWORD **2.** *Often* **Preface.** *Rom. Cath. Ch.* A thanksgiving prayer ending with the Sanctus and introducing the canon of the Mass.

So, with that definition in mind and considering this is not a missalette for Mass, I suppose this book should be introduced, and its scope and background explained. Oh, and I'll touch on the intention of it as well. The scope is broad. The background, well, (that's a deep subject), this is a collection of observations and thoughts I have jotted down over the past twenty years, with many relevant opinions added quite recently. The intention of this book—now that is something a little more difficult to explain. If I were to write the intention of this book is to sell enough copies to put at least one of my children through school, that would turn many people off. Therefore, I will declare at this moment, that is not the intention of this book.

Now that I have started a new paragraph, I can safely write the following: I would consider it beneficial to have the world's favor turning this book into a financial pleasure, although many of the opinions exposed herein may very well create the direct opposite response. Okay, back to completing the preface according to the definition above. The intention of this collection of thoughts, which have been put into essay form, is to make you think. This is a collection of my thoughts: bare, exposed, and uncensored. Naked to the world, for all to see, (or, in this case, read). Being in print does not make what is written right any more than it makes the thoughts and sentiments wrong. It does, however, give you, the reader, the experience of mentally agreeing or disagreeing with the ideas enclosed. By doing so, you will be, like it or not, *thinking* about the topics written in this book. The essays will also give you some insight into who I am (what a vain subject) as an individual. Hopefully, at least one copy will be around for my children to read, should they want to spend any additional time attempting to know their father a little better. As for my lovely wife, she already knows me and sticks around anyway.

Some of the essays will be controversial, some are lighthearted, but all are mine. As Andy Rooney wrote in his book *Not That You Asked*, "There's something in this book that will irritate almost everyone." No one could say it better than that.

Cheers,
James

"The third-rate mind is only happy when it is thinking with the majority. The second-rate mind is only happy when it is thinking with the minority. The first-rate mind is only happy when it is thinking."

—A. A. Milne

"Let's start the action!"

Frank Sinatra

In Loving Memory of Frank Bryant, Lee Fincannon, John Gigax, Justin Panides, Bert Price, Mary Price, Mark Magan, Bob Reynolds, and G. C. Wall.

For my wife, Barbara

AN IMMIGRATION SOLUTION

All right, here we go: A solution to the situation involving close to eleven million people living illegally within the borders of the United States. I offer this as a blueprint for our elected officials to use or build upon. Think of this as a proposal upon which the citizens of this country may vote. This is a plan for the federal government, since, at the moment, immigration is a federal, not a state, issue. The plan will require some preparation before implementation, which should be expected for such an arduous undertaking.

Also, it is important to read the entire plan before adopting an opinion. As I stated, this plan may be built upon or changed as needed. It is also important to keep an open mind while reading and not be put off by words such as "processing" or "registration." Every citizen of the United States, naturally born or naturalized, has gone through such a thing. Think about it: if you were born here, your parents had to fill out all sorts of paperwork and forms in order for you to be "registered." Furthermore, this plan does not grant amnesty. Illegals will not be granted citizenship. Please reread those last two sentences. For those citizens who want "retribution," there will be a form of "punishment." It will be explained. So, now that I have basically written a disclaimer, let's get to it. Please read the entire plan.

Persons living illegally within the United States must present themselves to immigration authorities. Yes, I said it, but stay with me. The illegal aliens will not be deported when they present themselves, and this will be guaranteed by the federal government. (Yes, a federal government guarantee may not carry a lot of weight right now, but it needs to in this case.) When the illegal aliens present themselves, they can expect a registration process similar to what one goes through at the DMV (but probably not as painful)—A complete background check, a photograph, and hopefully the issuance of a card. Afterward, these individuals will basically become what we called when I was a Border Patrol Agent, "lapper", LAPR (Lawfully Admitted for Permanent Residence).

The initial group of LAPRs will eventually decrease in number. This will not be a permanent status. This is a one-time status for a specific group of individuals (approximately eleven million). As the group ages and dies, this status will no longer be necessary. It is necessary for only one generation.

If the illegal aliens do not present themselves and they are found in the United States illegally, they will be deported. Period. Whether they have children who are citizens or not, they will be processed and deported just the same as if they had been caught at the border.

All illegal aliens will have the opportunity to present themselves with no reprisal. Therefore, there is no reason not to present themselves for registration. This goes for those seeking asylum, illegals, anyone. If they do not present themselves and are caught, they will be deported. It is important that the federal government carry this out immediately.

Once the illegal aliens are processed and registered, the following will take place: If they are not criminals (i.e., they have not committed any crimes other than illegal entry), they will no longer be illegal aliens. They will be aliens lawfully admitted for permanent residence.

This group of aliens will never be permitted to become US citizens. This is important. Because they broke the law, they cannot become citizens. They will not be entitled to Social Security or welfare benefits. However, they will be required to have payroll taxes deducted from their paycheck and pay all other taxes. This is the punishment I mentioned earlier. The punishment is they will help support Social Security and other social programs, but they cannot benefit from them and they cannot become citizens and all that entails, including the right to vote. If they do not agree to this, or if they think it is unfair, they are free to return to their country. It will be their choice. I think this is a fair way to handle the situation. All sides should be satisfied with it. It provides social justice, social benefit, and a positive outcome for all decent persons.

Some other issues:

You must be gainfully employed to remain in status. Australia has a similar immigration policy. I do not think minimum wage should apply to LAPRs. If someone has a farm, and a LAPR is willing to work for two dollars an hour, fine. If we are going to require employers to follow tax laws, it would be unfair to have them pay workers (who used to be undocumented and paid under the table) the current minimum wage. The law could be changed to have the minimum wage apply only to US citizens. Otherwise, you may end up paying twenty dollars for a head of lettuce.

A question which must be answered is what to do with minor children who are United States Citizens whose parents cannot obtain legal status. Whatever the answer, simply having children mustn't grant any type of waiver to any adult who otherwise would not be eligible to stay in the country.

Any company, enterprise, or person found to be employing an illegal alien will be fined a severe penalty, and the illegal employee will be deported. In my opinion, which this entire plan is, the penalty should be the same for companies and persons, whether they have deep pockets or not. The only way to ensure compliance is to make the punishment hurt.

Again, this plan can be used as a starting point. I only ask the American people and their elected officials to read and consider this plan as a possible solution.

To sum up: Illegals can turn themselves in or go home to their own country. After a background check, they will be lawfully admitted for permanent residence (LAPRs). They will never be permitted to become US citizens. They will pay payroll taxes funding Social Security and social programs, but they will never be allowed to receive Social Security benefits or welfare. If they do not turn themselves in and they are caught, they will be deported. Companies or persons found to be employing illegals will be fined, and the illegals will be deported.

They will not be eligible for any type of social programs, such as welfare. If they cannot maintain a livelihood, their legal status will be revoked and they will be deported. Minor children brought illegally into the country will have a path to citizenship, as long as they do not commit criminal acts and their parents are legally in the country. So there you have it, a solution to the immigration problem.

Some other things to consider: *What if the illegal alien does not/cannot obtain legal status but has minor children who are US citizens?* Whatever the answer is, the plan must not allow illegal aliens who cannot obtain legal status the ability to remain in the country. Simply having children must not grant a waiver. *What do we do with illegal aliens in local, state, and federal prisons?* First, if they are not imprisoned for violent crimes, why not deport them? Why are we, taxpayers, paying for their food, shelter, medical and dental care, and often college education? Kick them out. Send them back. Second, if they are imprisoned for violent crimes and it is decided to keep them incarcerated for their sentence, they should be deported immediately upon release.

MARRIAGE/GAY MARRIAGE

Why exactly is marriage a federal issue? That is the question I have when the topic of gay marriage is brought up. It is an extremely controversial topic which you should never bring up toward the end of an evening's discussion. What jurisdiction does the federal government have? Well, (that is a deep subject), I'll tell you. First, you must realize there are two very distinct schools of thought with regard to the US Constitution. One school of thought maintains any authority not specifically granted to the federal government by the US Constitution falls unto the jurisdiction and authority of the states. The other school of thought maintains any authority not specifically prohibited by the federal government to oversee by the US Constitution is fair game. The US Constitution states the following:

"The powers not delegated to the United States (federal government) by the Constitution, nor prohibited by it to the States, are reserved to the States respectively; or to the people."
This is the Tenth Amendment (Amendment X).

The way I interpret the above is, if the issue at hand is not specified for the feds to oversee, let the states or local communities handle it.

So I will ask again: why is the federal government concerning itself with marriage?

Marriage

The question to ask yourself is: what is marriage to you? Is marriage a legal status governed by the state? Or is marriage a spiritual sacrament governed by the Church? I ask because it is important to understand what exactly you are arguing about.

A good friend of mine just realized that marriage could be both. She was married by a priest, and she and her husband also filled out the required forms for the state. However, she did not go through all the steps before marriage required by the Catholic Church, which meant the Church did not recognize her marriage. To have her marriage recognized by the Church, even though it was already recognized by the state, she and her husband had to fill out several forms, attend some classes, have a few meetings with the priest, and then renew their vows. Now according to the state, her marriage is legal, and she and her husband have all the civil benefits associated with being married. But the Church did not consider the marriage legitimate and had additional requirements. It was important to her to have the marriage recognized by the Church, so they did what the Church required. It was also important to them that the marriage was recognized by the state; therefore, she took the steps the state required.

So I will ask again: what is marriage to you? As it now stands, it can be both. A Church and a state matter. It also should be noted that neither of these has sway over the other. If you are married by a priest and the priest doesn't sign the proper state forms and the forms are not submitted in the proper manner, the state will not recognize the marriage. Conversely, if you are married in a courthouse by a judge, your church may not recognize the marriage. Because of this, many need to complete the requirements for both institutions in order for the marriage to be validated by both.

Now let's turn to the issue termed "gay marriage." Because of the first and ninth amendments, I do not feel the federal government can order a church to change any of its sacraments. The Catholic Church will not allow people of the same gender to be married, so that should end the spiritual debate. Now if citizens vote to allow people of the same sex to be married under the requirements of the state, or vote to not allow people of the same sex to be married under the requirements of the state, that should end the debate of legality. Only it didn't.

For example, in California, the issue was put to the voters as Proposition 8, and the voters voted "no." Now, because the vote was appealed and reversed by the Ninth Circuit, the issue is with the Supreme Court. In my opinion, the Supreme Court should overturn the Ninth Circuit ruling, because the question was put up in a legal manner, a vote was held by the residents of the state of California in a legal manner, and the votes were counted in a legal manner. The will of the people was counted and declared. The declaration was "no."

This was a vote to change the State's Constitution. It didn't pass.

If some of the people of the state did not like the outcome of the vote, they should put it up for a vote again. This is how our country is supposed to work. The people make their voices heard, either by direct voting or through their representatives. The result of the vote should never have been overturned by the Ninth Circuit, and the issue should never have made it all the way to the Supreme Court. I hope the Supreme Court does not make a ruling on this and sends it back to the state. Should they feel the need to make a ruling, I hope they overturn the Ninth Circuit ruling and return this back to the state. Should they uphold the ruling, well, (that's a deep subject), they will prove that the will of the people does not matter.

So, why exactly is gay marriage a federal issue? And if it is a federal issue, as long as the government does not try to impose rules upon religious institutions, what does it matter to me? I already understand marriage as defined by two separate institutions with two separate sets of requirements. I am Catholic. The Catholic Church will not authorize same-sex marriage: Fine with me. If another religion wants to authorize same-sex marriage, it does not matter to me, because I am Catholic.

If the people want to vote and want to allow same-sex couples to have the same legal rights as married couples, it will not have any impact upon me, my family, or my church. Call it a civil union, call it marriage, call it bondage, call it prison—I don't care. My church defines marriage one way. As long as my church is not forced by the government to do something contrary to its teachings, it will not have any effect upon me or my family.

Let the states or communities vote on the issue, and let the vote stand. If you do not like the outcome of the vote, move somewhere where there are more like-minded people, where the vote is more in line with your way of thinking. Just don't make this a federal issue. It is my hope that the Supreme Court will not make this a federal issue. However, by the time you read this, a decision may have already been made.

DON'T JUST ARM YOUR SONS; ARM YOUR DAUGHTERS AS WELL

There is something very frightening about new legislation which has been introduced in Congress and now has been referred to Committee. (Though, it could be argued that any legislation that makes its way through Congress is frightening.)

The issue to be discussed in this essay involves women in combat. Yes, I thought I would write about a light and easy topic, nothing too heavy or polarizing. Now I am not going to spend any words on the merits or physiological impact of having women in a combat unit (no words except those I just wrote). I want to write about a more appalling issue, as a result of this new legislation.

The issue I find so disturbing in *H.R. 747 is, as written, it will make my daughters eligible for the draft, should there ever be a need for another. Yes, you read that correctly. H.R. 747 will require women, as well as men, between the ages of 18 and 25 to register with the Selective Service. Let me re-write this again, because I do not think this was the intent of any person arguing the merits of whether a woman was capable of serving in a combat unit; nor do I think it was the intent of any person arguing a woman's right to serve her country in the same manner as a man, should be prevented from doing so. I do not think that was their intent, yet the result has the 113th Congress in the First Session presenting HR 747. To quote the HR 747, this means to "amend the Military Selective Service Act to require the registration of women with the Selective Service System in light of the Department of Defense elimination of the rule excluding women from direct ground combat assignments in the Armed Forces."

___

* H.R.747 and H.R.748 are located in the Appendix of this book.

Let me write that again, "…to require the registration of women with the Selective Service System…"

I have two daughters. I also have a son. I come from a military family. My family has been in this country before it was a nation. Both of my grandfathers served in the military. My father served, and my wife's father served in the military. My wife was a Naval Nurse. I served in the military. My point of that little piece of family history is I believe in serving your Country. I also believe our men are our warriors, and if necessary, even my newborn son. Although I promised I would not write anything about my opinion when it comes to women in combat, I am persuaded for the sake of argument and this essay to acknowledge the right of a woman to serve alongside a man should she volunteer to do so. However, I oppose women being required to register for the draft.

There is more to the bill and there is even a "Presidential Guarantee" in section 109 which I will let you read for yourself as I will add H.R.747 and HR 748 IH in the appendix.

The point I want to make is this: I never thought the United States of America would require by law the women of this great nation to register with the Selective Service. This bill lays the groundwork to require women to serve in combat. This bill should not be allowed to pass, and should this bill pass, we should demand it be repealed.

Allow To Volunteer – Do Not Demand Requirement

This is another reason for you, the reader, should call your **representative.

** The current name and number of every congressman and senator are located in the appendix of this book.

HATE CRIMES

The fact the federal government can bring charges against anyone based upon what someone *thinks* should scare every single one of you. The crime itself should be enough for indictment, and the penalties should reflect the severity of the crime. Aren't assault and murder heinous enough? How much more egregious can you get? Every assault, every murder, every act of arson is a hate crime ... isn't it? Motivation is something a prosecutor uses to prove guilt: *motive*. The motive is oftentimes related to the penalty. Isn't that enough? If the penalties are not severe enough, make them more severe for every case.

The definition of a *hate crime* from the FBI's website is

> A hate crime is a traditional offense like murder, arson, or vandalism with an added element of bias. For the purposes of collecting statistics, Congress has defined a hate crime as a "criminal offense against a person or property motivated in whole or in part by an offender's bias against a race, religion, disability, ethnic origin or sexual orientation." Hate itself is not a crime—and the FBI is mindful of protecting freedom of speech and other civil liberties.

The FBI website also states the following:

> A hate crime is not a distinct federal offense. However, the federal government can and does investigate and prosecute crimes of bias as civil rights violations, which do fall under its jurisdiction. These efforts serve as a

11

backstop for state and local authorities, which handle the vast majority of hate crime cases. A 1994 federal law also increased penalties for offenses proven to be hate crimes.

In 2009, the passage of a new law—the first significant expansion of federal criminal civil rights law since the mid-1990s—gave the federal government the authority to prosecute violent hate crimes, including violence and attempted violence directed at the gay, lesbian, bisexual, and transgender community, to the fullest extent of its jurisdiction. The Matthew Shepard and James Byrd, Jr., Hate Crimes Prevention Act also provides funding and technical assistance to state, local, and tribal jurisdictions to help them to more effectively investigate, prosecute, and prevent hate crimes.

Now, as a special agent myself and a member of the Federal Law Enforcement Officers Association (FLEOA), I am not speaking against my fellow law enforcement officers or any aspect of their job. I simply want you, the reader, to have the official language and definition of the law—a law I believe is flawed and dangerous.

- A crime is a crime. Assault is assault. Murder is murder.
- How can anyone, even the government, know what an individual is thinking?
- This law should be scary to everyone. Not only does it allow the federal government to bring charges on cases where they would otherwise not have jurisdiction, but this sets a precedent that the government can charge you based upon what you are thinking.

Once again, every assault is a hate crime, isn't it? So why do we need a special law—a law to make murder more of a murder?

One more thing: Hate crimes charges also seem to be applied unfairly and one sided. For instance, there was recently an incident in Florida in which three black teenagers were caught on film beating up a white teenager on a school bus. The teenagers were charged with assault. Now, if three white teenagers had beaten up a black teenager, how do you think they would have been charged? Seriously?

If you think this law should be repealed, call your *representative.

---

* The current name and number of every congressman and senator are located in the appendix of this book.

EGYPT

Just a thought: Our foreign policy states if a coup occurs within a nation, to whom (the United States) provide aid (money), the foreign aid shall stop. Why are we still providing aid to Egypt? Just for reference, the definition of a *coup* is

> "a sudden overthrow of a government in deliberate violation of constitutional forms by a group of persons in or previously in positions of authority."

Isn't that what is taking place in Egypt right now? Aren't we (the United States) in serious financial trouble? Why are we (the United States) not following through with our own foreign policy? How can we (the United States) expect the world to respect us, trust us, or even fear us if we do not follow through with our own policies?

If you agree with me, this is another reason for you, the reader, to call your *representative.

---

* The current name and number of every congressman and senator are located in the appendix of this book.

ANNIVERSARY

The year 2013 is the one hundred–year anniversary of the Sixteenth Amendment.

The code which enforces the amendment began as a few pages, now has more words than:

- the Bible,
- the complete works of Tolstoy,
- the complete works of Dostoevsky, and
- the complete works of Shakespeare

Combined! That is right, *combined*!

If you do not know what the Sixteenth Amendment is, look it up.

MAIN STREET

When you hear about the middle class or Main Street America, does it annoy you just a little? It seems so irresponsible to place such a diverse and large portion of the country into one category. I just completed my taxes. Actually, I just paid an accountant to complete my taxes, and I was shocked to find out I had moved into a higher tax bracket. I was shocked because I am a federal government employee who has been subject to the pay freeze for the past two years. So how is it possible the government considers my income to have risen enough to move me into a higher tax bracket? I even had another child during the year, adding another dependent. Everything is costing me more. My salary hasn't increased, yet my taxes went up. I am certain I am not the only person in this or a similar situation. Our tax regulations are ridiculous. Furthermore, I do not think you could find anyone who would disagree with that statement. So why isn't something being done to change it?

Do the members of the House and the Senate even know what a gallon of milk costs? More to the point, do they have a need to care? Notice I didn't write, "Do they even care?" But do they have a need? I know what a gallon of milk costs, and I also know this week a gallon of milk at Walgreens is $1.35 cheaper than at Publix or Giant or Safeway. I have a need to care, because costs keep rising and I live on a budget.

As I write this, it is important to point out another fact which is often misused or misinterpreted. When you hear about "tax loopholes," please remember these are not illegal. In fact, they shouldn't be referred to as "loopholes." They are part of the regulations just like child deductions or deductible charitable contributions.

Loophole as defined in *Webster's II New Riverside University Dictionary* is

> "a way of escaping a difficulty, esp. an ambiguity or omission, as in the wording of a contract or law, that provides a means of evasion."
>
> That definition does not seem to fit with the way it is often used when many in the media are discussing our tax regulations. Not everyone is evading the regulations, some are simply following the law as written and taking advantage of the exemptions available.

I just wanted to point that out.

PEANUTS

No, this is not an essay about the beloved Charles Schulz characters and comic strip, which is still running in the newspapers, and the cartoons are still broadcast on television every Halloween, Thanksgiving, and Christmas. Though, perhaps in the future, I will write an essay about how those characters have remained relevant for so many years. But, unfortunately, this is a much more important and serious subject. Sorry.

My eldest daughter has a peanut and tree nut allergy. My lovely wife and I are hoping she grows out of it. We are told it can happen and is common. But for now we deal with the reality our daughter can go into anaphylactic shock if she is exposed to peanuts or tree nuts. If you don't know what I am talking about, I'm not surprised. Before we found out about her allergy, I never realized how dangerous the condition can be. It is life-threating!

Two events occurred, which I read about in the newspaper. One was before my daughter was born, and one happened after she was diagnosed with the allergy. I am writing about them to illustrate how different my reaction was to them. It is amazing how involved we become when something affects us personally.

In the local newspaper, there was a story about a group of middle school students, (There is no longer Junior High-school. If you know what I am talking about, you just "dated yourself".), who had spread peanut butter over the latches of most of the lockers in the hallway of the school. When I read the article, I remember thinking to myself, *What a mess that will be to clean up*, and I wondered what prompted that prank. Again, this was before my daughter was born.

Later, a few years after my daughter was born, I read a story in the local paper about a playground that had peanut butter smeared all over the playground equipment. Anger was my reaction. *Don't these people realize they could kill someone?* That was all I could think about. The incident was no longer just a prank. It was a potential assault!

After calming down, all I could think about was if I could ever let my little girl play at a public playground again. Was I going to need to wipe down every surface of every playground just to make certain it was safe before I let her be a kid? Or was I going to keep my little girl away from all of the tax-funded playgrounds and wrap her in a cocoon? Obviously, neither option was plausible or realistic. So my lovely wife and I killed her ... just kidding. Seriously, that was only a terrible joke inserted to illicit a certain response in order to make light of a serious issue. My eldest daughter is alive and well. However we do need to always carry an *EpiPpen with us wherever we go, just in case she is exposed to peanuts or tree nuts. (*Trademark name for the epinephrine medicine we carry around with us.)

If you or your child has a food allergy, Food Allergy Research & Education (FARE) has created a notification card you can download from their website to give to servers at restaurants. It isn't the only thing you need to protect your child, but it is a start.

THAT TIME OF YEAR

The Christmas season is once again upon us. Notice I did not write the "holiday season." That is because I am a Christian—Catholic, to draw it down further—so to me it is the Christmas season. (By the way, the word *holiday* literally means "holy day.".) The fact I refer to this time of year as the Christmas season does not mean I am against any other religion. If one wants to refer to this time of year as the Hanukkah season, fine with me. To be honest, I do not really care. I do not care because it does not affect my life or my family. The only time someone else's opinion has any effect on another's day-to-day life is when intolerance and stubbornness come into the picture. Yes, stubbornness. Like a petulant child. Why should anyone in this country care about what other people put on their front lawn to celebrate a certain time of year? Is a manger scene really offensive to anyone? Really? How could two adults standing over a child's crib be offensive?

Another point about this time of year is that it is a federal holiday. Yes, Christmas is a *federal holiday. It is a day off, just like Thanksgiving, Martin Luther King, Jr. Day, Columbus Day, New Year's Day, President's Day, Memorial Day, Veterans Day, and Labor Day. Are any of those days offensive or religious? So one could make the argument that Christmas is not a religious holiday, but a federal one. I said one could *make* the argument; I didn't say it was correct. But why should one need to argue

---

* In the strict sense, there are no National holidays in the United States. The President and Congress can legally designate federal holidays only for federal government employees.

   Each of the 50 states has jurisdiction over its holidays. However, most states observe the federal holidays.

about it in the first place? It is a day off work! Yeah! So who cares what or how anyone celebrates it?

Of course, some people do. And because this country is so great, everyone has a voice and a right to be heard, even if their voice is ridiculous and actually does to another what they claim is being done to them—infringing upon their rights as US citizens. (I point out US citizens, because if you are not a citizen or a legal permanent resident, you do not have a dog in this fight. So just be quiet before you are deported.)

When a judge rules that a person can or cannot do something, most likely someone's rights will be infringed upon. Because this country, as great as it is, has become a society of remonstrance and appeasement, judges often are forced to make controversial decisions. Wouldn't it be better if, when something becomes an issue, the town or community simply votes on it and the majority rules? If you don't like it, move to a town or community that is more in line with your views.

When in conflict, go to the source. When doing so, ask yourself, "Does the subject of my aggravation actually constitute a conflict which has an effect upon my life or my family?" Or, is it simply an aggravation? The difference is an aggravation is simply that, and it is something with which you can live. If it is more than that and has a negative impact on your life, freedom, or rights, then you have a conflict. When in conflict, go to the source. I will leave it up to you, the reader, to decide what or who the "source" is. Is it within yourself or the actions of another?

COLUMBUS DAY

The second Monday in October is Columbus Day. You remember Columbus. He is that vain, mentally questionable, white male scavenger oppressor from Spain (even though he wasn't Spanish). He is the one who received credit for all of those countries he didn't discover when he got lost.

That may as well be the story, considering what children are learning these days. (Hold on a second, I said "learning"—my mistake. We don't know if they are learning anything. I should have written, "being taught".) But what happened to the old Columbus? The one I learned about in grade school? The old Columbus who was the reason I got a day off from school? There is still a federal holiday, and some children still get out of school. But the reasons given to them by the controllers of political correctness aren't the same reasons I received. I can only imagine what teachers are saying about or being told to say about the Fourth of July. I can picture it now: It's the last day of school, mid-June, as opposed to the end of May. The children are eagerly awaiting the last bell to ring, which will announce summer break, so they can start their government-funded midnight basketball league designed to keep them off the streets and out of gangs. So they are sitting at their desks, and the history teacher (I'm surprised "history" hasn't been changed to "person-story".) says something along the lines of, "Keep in mind when the Fourth of July celebration and beer drinking begins, what you are really celebrating is the fact a bunch of undereducated white men didn't want to pay their taxes."

When the bell rings, the children begin their long-awaited two and a half months off from school. Then they will most likely go to a picnic, if the air quality isn't too bad, and drink from bottled water because the aquifer is so badly contaminated or simply dry. Maybe they will go to the beach for ten minutes—or longer if they wear SPF 2,000. But it is just as well. They couldn't barbecue or fly a kite or even surf at the beach any more anyway. Besides, syringes or oil from a spill may be on the shore. Or a beached whale, which no decent parent should let their child see because that may lead to a discussion about death. Not to mention Mom and Dad couldn't take the time off from their jobs to make the trip anyhow. So, if their parents can afford it, the children may go to a summer camp with an Indian—I mean Native American—name, to learn how their ancestors (white children now) were lying, dishonorable men. (Not women, mind you. The women were also victims, so none of history is their fault.) All of this is just in time for the Fourth of July, our country's official birthday celebration. To celebrate a country founded by those bigoted, hypocritical men of freedom who raped their slaves.

Ah, yes, what a proud heritage our children are being taught. But thank goodness for our blessings today. No longer must we be victims of the infractions of our civil rights. No longer are we prisoners, forced to pray to God Almighty in school. Thank goodness there is no longer a wasted three minutes of silence so those who want to pray can. How did we ever endure that oppression for so long? Not to mention the Pledge of Allegiance. Thank Go—I mean the maker. The maker of the laws—those pure, unimposing persons who are finally untwisting the words of our bigoted, sexist forefathers. Those evil men of God and liberty and justice.

COLUMBUS DAY: HAPPIER VERSION

It is just about that time of year again. Depending on where you live, the air begins to become a little cooler, just enough to tickle the back of your throat. Leaves, along with children's grades, begin to fall with the countdown to the holidays. Advertisers and merchants are starting to push Christmas items before Thanksgiving has arrived. Pumpkins are for sale now. In another five weeks or so, there will be a Christmas tree lot on just about every corner. Some mothers are making last-minute changes to Halloween costumes. Others have started to plan Thanksgiving dinner and send out invitations to parties. Fathers are mowing lawns, unless they have sons old enough to do it, for the last couple times this year. The chore, again depending upon where you live, will be replaced by raking fallen leaves. It is time to put away the shorts and take out the sweaters. Change your sandals or flip-flops for boots, and sunblock for scarves. (Speaking of boots, is it just me, or doesn't a woman wearing a skirt and boots in the winter time look stunning?)

Yes indeed, every year after Columbus Day things begin to change. It's a change which is usually welcome by all. It is happening now and will happen again. See you next year.

FLY YOUR FLAG/COLORS

Remember our veterans, and show your pride in our country by flying your flag on the following days throughout the year. Think of these days like holy days of obligation in the Catholic Church. You should try to display your national pride on these days. If you are not particularly proud of your nation at the moment, fly the nation's colors to display your desire to restore the honor of the nation, or to remember the women and men who sacrificed for this nation, for the idea of this nation, for the honor of this nation, for the integrity of this nation, for the children of this nation, and for the future of this Nation.

On June 22, 1942, Congress, in a joint resolution, advised the flag to be flown on certain days. (They have since updated the rules of displaying the flag.) The following list contains the days to display the flag in 2013. When necessary, I have noted the change in date for future years.

Inauguration Day: January 20
President's Day: February 18, 2013; February 17, 2014; February 16, 2015
VE Day: May 8
Armed Forces Day: May 18, 2013; May 17, 2014; May 16, 2015 (third Saturday in May)
Memorial Day: May 27, 2013; May 26, 2014; May 25, 2015 (remember, the flag is flown at half-mast until noon)
Flag Day: June 14
Independence Day: July 4
V-J Day: August 14
Labor Day: September 2, 2013; September 1, 2014; September 7, 2015 (first Monday)
Constitution Day: September 17

Patriot Day: September 11

POW/MIA Recognition Day: September 20, 2013; September 19, 2014; September 18, 2015

Columbus Day: the second Monday in October

Election Day: The first Tuesday in November.

Veterans Day: November 11

Pearl Harbor Day: December 7

If you know someone who made what many consider the ultimate sacrifice for this nation, honor that person by flying the flag on the day they died.

Frank Bryant: April 27

IMPORTANT/ OR AT LEAST INTERESTING DATES

Don't worry, I am not going to describe some of the evenings I shared with ladies before I met my lovely wife—though that subject may make for an interesting read. But I would probably need to change the names and restaurants and even cities to avoid lawsuits claiming defamation of character, which would basically make my life a living hell. Merely describing a lady being associated with me in a personal setting could result in accusations of calumny.

No need for you or me to worry about any of that. This essay involves yet another little aspect of life I find interesting. I could have just written that this essay involves yet another topic of useless knowledge, but then you may have stopped reading. You may have stopped already, unless you are reading this word, and this word—okay, I will stop, so you will not stop reading. This essay involves what my lovely wife describes as useless knowledge that will only help if you find yourself on *Jeopardy!*

The day events took place is the subject, and I will list some important, or at least interesting, ones. Let me explain how I came across these and started collecting them. Several years ago, my mother, Linda, started sending me calendars for Christmas. Now, don't think to yourself, *Wow, a calendar, I can barely contain my excitement*. Although that may have been my initial reaction. However, I soon discovered my mother had spent a lot of time on these calendars. You see, every year, she writes down important events on the dates they took place, and she also notes the year. She also chooses a calendar with subject matter I would find interesting. For instance, this past year the calendar showcased antique maps. Another year it was the *Sports Illustrated* swimsuit calendar. You get the drift. So every year, she takes the time to pick out calendars and then write important events, including the birthdays and anniversaries of family members, on the dates, which is very helpful to my lovely wife, to whom I have delegated the responsibility of mailing birthday cards, making phone calls, and such social responsibilities and etiquette.

So, without spending any more time describing what a meaningful gift my mother sends me each year, I will list some of the important dates she has notated over the years. I will leave out the birthdays of my family (you're welcome). In fact, I will leave out all birthdays, except that of Frank Sinatra. He was born on December 12. The list of dates can be found in the Appendix under "Important/Interesting Dates." Cheers.

LIGHT A GRILL LIKE YOU MEAN IT

My Uncle Mark is quite a fellow. I often refer to him as my favorite uncle, or F. U. Should you have the pleasure of being invited to his home, odds are you will be welcome to stay for dinner. The meal will involve something grilled or smoked, and you can be assured it will be excellent. (Of course, being invited to dinner assumes you make it through the door. If he doesn't find your company pleasing, then you will not make it through the door. You may not make it into the driveway because of the chain, but that is for another time.)

On one of my many visits to his home, the invitation to dinner came and the grill needed to be lit. On this particular visit he showed me a method of lighting a grill (or smoker) that I have used ever since. Not only does it not involve lighter fluid, which some say leaves an unpleasant taste on the food (I have never been able to tell), but this is simply the coolest method I have ever seen. (I realize using the adjective "coolest" to describe lighting a fire seems odd, but this is really cool.) It takes grilling to an entirely new level of manliness.

To start, you go ahead and place the charcoal, as you normally would, for whatever method of grilling you are planning to use (i.e., direct, indirect, whatever). It also doesn't matter what type of charcoal you are using (briquettes or lump); as long as you are using charcoal, you are in the right state of mind and you are actually grilling. If you are not using charcoal (or wood), you can stop reading this and go back to your *cooking* in your outdoor kitchen.

After you have the charcoal arranged as you want it (this is where it gets amazing, and anyone watching will realize you are going to light this grill like you mean it), go ahead and grab your blowtorch. Yes, that is right, I said *blowtorch*. One that uses a small propane cylinder is fine; in fact, that is the type my uncle uses. Light the blowtorch (using the striker or whatever), and direct that awesome display of intense heat at one side or in the middle of your pile of charcoal. A surprisingly short time later, your grill will be lit. If you started on one side and are not quite ready to put away the awesome display of manhood, you can always light the other side.

Just remember when you are all finished, every single one of your friends and neighbors will tell you how cool that was and ask where you learned how to do that. If you want to give proper credit, when asked where you learned how to light a grill this way, you can respond, "F. U."

A CHILI RECIPE

There are several recipes for chili, and everyone swears his or hers is the best, is the most authentic, won the awards, was passed down from the pioneers in their family, won as payment in a poker game, was stolen from "Cookie"—whatever. I personally have several recipes, and if this book turns out to be a financial success, I will gladly release another recipe in this book's sequel. In the meantime, I want to share this particular recipe with you. I learned it while living on the Texas/Mexico border town of Laredo. I spent quite a few years there and learned quite a bit. Believe it or not, while in Laredo, I spent a lot of time actually working, though you would not know that should you happen to look at my photo albums from those years. All right, I believe that is enough setup, so let's just get to it.

There are several things you will need before getting started. It may not all make sense at first, but read the entire recipe, follow the directions, and it will all come together. And remember, cooking is not baking. Baking is like math. Cooking is like sex. You have to feel your way through it—a nudge here, a pinch there, and always pay attention.

For the fire:
Mesquite wood chips and hardwood charcoal

For the rub:
2–3 cloves of garlic
Chili powder
Cayenne pepper
1/4 cup Coke
1/4 cup Texas beer

31

For the radio:
Blues, preferably Texas blues like Stevie Ray Vaughan or his brother, or even The Fabulous Thunderbirds

For the cooler:
Texas beer, like Shiner Bock, or even a cheaper one, like Lone Star

Other Ingredients:
2 lbs. chuck roast
Salt to taste
2–3 cloves garlic
1/4 cup Coke
Juice of one lime
Olive Oil
1 12-oz beer
Chili powder
8-oz can tomato sauce
Cayenne pepper
14-oz diced tomatoes (canned or fresh)
Black pepper
16-oz kidney beans (if canned, drain)
1/2 tsp. cumin
Any fiery chilies to bring up the heat, as desired
1/2 tsp. oregano
1/2 tsp. paprika

Let's get started. Turn on the music, and open a cold beer.

The chuck roast should be as lean as possible and at least three inches thick. A couple hours before you plan to make the chili, rub the meat with the crushed garlic, salt, chili powder, and cayenne pepper. Put it in a gallon-size zip-lock bag, along with the Coke and 1/4 cup beer, and place in the refrigerator. Turn and shake it every thirty minutes.

Fire up enough hardwood charcoal in a grill (preferably one with a cover) to sear the meat. At the same time, soak a few handfuls of mesquite chips in one part water and three parts beer. (The beer may not actually add any additional flavor to the smoke, but it looks "exotic" should anyone be watching you cook.) When the coals are covered with ash, spread them out evenly and scatter the soaked mesquite chips evenly over them. Then immediately set the meat on the grill over the smoke about an inch from the coals. Cover the grill, and adjust the dampers to maintain a slow, steady heat. Let the meat sear for no more than ten minutes. (This is meant to flavor the meat, not to cook it.) Turn the meat over for about the same amount of time, then remove from the heat and transfer to the fridge to let it cool for about an hour.

After the meat has cooled, trim away any surface fat or cartilage. With a sharp knife, cube the meat into the smallest pieces you have the patience for, saving all the juices. (Believe me when I tell you to cut the meat into the smallest pieces you have the patience for. The end result will be worth the possible backache from bending over the cutting board.)

Heat olive oil in a large, heavy pot over moderate heat. Stir in garlic, and sauté. Stir in the meat and all of the reserved meat juices. Add the seasonings and the tomatoes, stirring and tasting along the way. Crumble in the fiery peppers to bring up the heat to taste; however, try not to adjust the seasoning to perfection now. The long cooking will smooth and sweeten it.

Lower the heat as low as possible. If the pot is left to boil, the meat will be tough. After the first hour, every half an hour or so, taste for seasoning, adjusting and thickening with mesa (flour) a teaspoon at a time. The chili should be ready to eat in three hours, though sitting in the fridge overnight always seems to make it taste better.

Serve the chili simmering in large heavy bowls with a chunk of sturdy bread for dipping and a side of beans, but not much else—except maybe black coffee or quart-sized glasses of sweet tea or a few bottles of your favorite beer. Oh, don't forget the hot sauce. After a while of eating with friends, utter the words of a controversial subject, lean back in your chair, and start arguing.

ROUTINE

Below is an old routine written and performed many times over. Grab a friend, memorize your part, and have fun. Your friend may balk at first, but when you run into them, in a bar, and you haven't seen them for a while and you pull this out, you will thank me.

erson 1: "You remind me of a babe."
Person 2: "What babe?"
Person 1: "The babe with the power."
Person 2: "What power?"
Person 1: "The power of who do."
Person 2: "Who do?"
Person 1: "You do."
Person 2: "I do what?"
Person 1: "You remind me of a babe."

Continue for as long as your partner will let you.

Sometimes it is the simple things that can bring amusement or annoyance.

IT'S SIMPLE, KNOT

How to Tie a Bowline

- Form a small loop, leaving enough rope for the loop size you want.
- Pass the end of the rope through the loop.
- Continue around the longer end of the rope and then back through the hole.
- Pull.

There is also the "chasing the rabbit around the tree and into the rabbit hole" description, which is actually the same thing. If you are having trouble, look at the image below while reading the instructions.

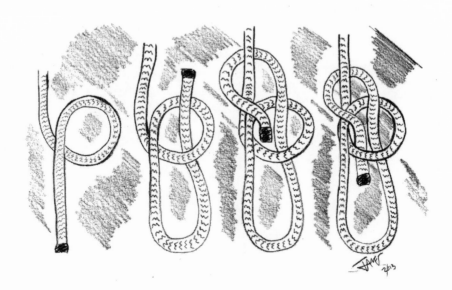

Slip Knot

Many people confuse the bowline knot with a slip knot because it *slips*. However, the slip knot is completely different. The slip knot is a temporary knot which can be quickly untied by simply pulling on the short end of the rope.

To tie a slip knot, form a loop at the end of the rope.

Pinch the long end of the rope into a V shape ("bite"), tuck it into the loop.

Tighten.

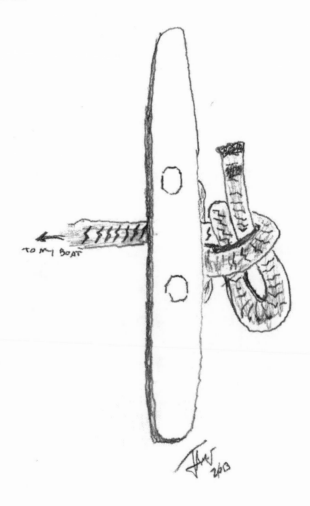

How to Tie the Knot/Get Married

First, don't—unless, of course, you have found the girl of your dreams, are completely and totally in love with her, and care for her wants more than your own ... or if she is independently wealthy and will put up with all of your nonsense.

I am not certain how it works for ladies, but for men, or at least for me, it went like this. After years of dating different women, you begin to learn more about yourself and how/what you may need and desire from a potential wife. I learned that I am pretty demanding and often shallow, but I have the capacity to be quite charming.

Before even considering marriage, there must be something there, whatever that *something* is (even if it is physical attractiveness). Now, many will say that is shallow, but I disagree. Anyone who says the appearance of their partner doesn't really matter is, in my opinion, lying. Of course physical attraction is important. In many instances it is the first thing that brings said person to your attention. You *noticed* them. Now, I am not saying physical attractiveness is the most important thing to look for, but it is important for most people—unless there is money involved. (That was written facetiously. Relax.) There must be something more, because as we age, our physical beauty may diminish, but having a hottie is a great place to start.

In the end, you should be able to put her wants and needs before you own. (She should also be able to do the same thing.) Realistically that will not always happen, because we are human and can be selfish. When it does happen, that is when you have marital bliss.

Now, in today's society, many of the social etiquettes of the past have changed. Take asking for permission from a lady's father before proposing. Divorce, step-parents, bitterness, can make what used to be a respectful gesture a train wreck. However, if all is well with your future bride's family, go for it. If he drinks, ask him to meet you for a cocktail, perhaps before a planned "family dinner" out. If that doesn't work, find another location, but keep the following three simple rules in mind. 1. Make certain it is just the two of you in a public place. Don't pull him aside at the Thanksgiving dinner table. 2. Keep it simple. A place where you can have a relatively quick conversation. You do not want to ask permission over a round of golf; that could lead to a very long afternoon. 3. Make certain you pick up the tab. For a bonus, do not let your potential bride know. She will find out later and everyone will feel special.

THE RULE

You are on a cellular phone call, and the call is "dropped" for whatever reason. That is not the annoying part. The annoying part is when you call the person back, only to be directed to their voice mail, because they also are attempting to call you back. This can go on for several minutes, until both of you give up and check the voice messages later and, in many cases, forget what you were talking about in the first place. Annoying.

I have a solution. I want you to share this with everyone you interact with.

Call it "The Rule".

Here we go. If you are on a call and the call is "dropped", the person who initiated the original phone call is the person who calls back. Got it? It is that simple. Share it. As Barney would say, "make it a thing." Remember, it is The Rule.

BEWARE WHAT YOU WEAR

"Toga! Toga! Toga!" Anyone who has seen the movie *Animal House* knows this scene and can probably recite most of it. The movie had a lasting effect, in that a toga party is almost a requirement for anyone attending college. However, should you be in college and have time to read this book (or what I used to call "entertainment reading") and are female, you should be aware of the following fact. If you are older, like me, the following information may no longer be useful, but it may make you remember a time in your life when shouting, "Toga! Toga! Toga!" was not only appropriate, but expected.

Togas were unique to Rome and were worn by free-born Roman men and as a mark of distinction. Ironically, the only women who wore togas were prostitutes, because they were not allowed to wear stolas.

Ladies, think of this at your next toga party. You may send the wrong message to those in the know. Or perhaps, if you wear one, you are sending the right message. Only you know.

TOILET

If there are only three urinals in a public restroom, and there is no one else there, why do some men choose the middle urinal? Are they hoping someone will enter and have to stand next to them? If given the chance, I prefer not to stand next to someone while using the facilities. Therefore, if I enter the restroom and there are three urinals I will choose one on the end. But that is just me.

And for goodness' sake, stay off the phone while you are in here. That is disgusting. Show some pride. Display a little dignity. Have a little modesty.

The following quiz is for men. Just for practice, take the quiz below. Choose what you think is the best urinal to use.

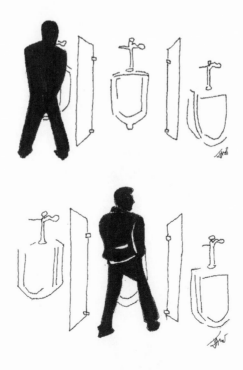

SELF-TEST

You are standing on top of a building. It does not really matter how tall the building is (four stories, ten stories, whatever), as long as the height is significant. There is another building of equal height just across the street, and a sturdy platform is laid across, connecting the two buildings. Let's say the plank is twelve inches wide. Got it?

Okay, answer the following questions as honestly as you can. If someone offered you one dollar to walk across, would you? What if you were offered ten dollars? Would that change your mind? All right, how about twenty? No wait, how about one hundred dollars? Would that be enough to entice you? If not, how much money would it take for you to risk your life to walk across?

Did you answer? If you did, you just put a price on your life. You just told yourself how much you think your life is worth. (Didn't see that one coming, did you?) If you answered no amount of money would be enough, you just learned something about yourself (even if it is something as simple as you are afraid of heights). If you backtrack and now tell yourself you would do it just for the challenge because you believe in your abilities and like to take risks; you should have answered that you would do it for a dollar, because if it was truly about the challenge, the amount of money wouldn't matter.

There is no right or wrong answer. This is a self-test.

JUST FOR CLARIFICATION

There are many misconceptions people have concerning various subjects. Some are simple mistakes, and others are just completely wrong due to ignorance. Perhaps institutions of education are not teaching the proper meaning or the original definition of certain things. Or perhaps society as a whole has simply forgotten them. Hopefully the next few pages will clear up some of the topics. I have decided to use the original definitions to avoid conflict. The intention being, that if you know where the word/ concept originated, you can decide for yourself if the new definition/ explanation is appropriate. The idea for this particular essay was inspired by a conversation I had with my younger brother, a college student working on his PhD. For some reason, the term "third world country" came up, which he described as poor, underdeveloped country with very little infrastructure (e.g., no running water). When I heard his "definition" a blood vessel in my head almost burst. Soon after, my lovely wife came into the room and I asked her to define a "third world country" and she responded in a similar fashion, I believe the blood vessel did burst.

Please feel free to look these things up for yourself. In the event I am wrong, please let me know.*

The Random House College Dictionary defines *third world* as "the group of developing nations, especially, of Asia and Africa, that do not align themselves with or are not committed to, the policies of either the United Stated or the Soviet Union."

First world was considered the United States.

Second world was considered the Soviet Union.

---

* You may e-mail me at the following address: ajumbleofthoughts@writeme.com

Nowhere was the notion of no infrastructure or impoverishment mentioned or inferred. It basically meant those nations which did not aligned themselves with the Capitalists or the Communists.

Now that the Soviet Union no longer exists, one could argue the definition of second world needs to be changed. If so, perhaps the definition of first world and third world also should be changed. But until that time, I implore you not to go around stating the bit about no infrastructure and impoverished and whatever.

Food Is "Done," People Are "Finished"

One shouldn't say, "I'm done," at the dinner table upon completing a meal. The correct statement is "I'm finished." A roast or a cake is *done* when cooked. You stick a fork in it to see if it is *done*. The expression "Stick a fork in me, I'm done" points out "done" refers to food. So remember—and for goodness sake, teach your children and anyone else who will listen—food is done. People are finished.

Trousers: Cuffs or No Cuffs

If trousers have a cuff—a portion at the end, folded up, often sewn on the side of the legs to hold in place—those trousers are to be worn in the daytime. If they do not have a cuff, they are considered to be more formal and may be worn in the evening and at night. This is why you will never see a pair of tuxedo trousers with cuffs. (Note, trousers without cuffs may also be worn during the day.)

Our Government

We do not live in a democracy. We live in a representative republic.

No Hazard Lights While Driving in the Rain

When it is raining, even if it is raining extremely hard, do not turn on your hazard lights! **First, it is illegal in many states. Second, you can cause more accidents, because the hazard lights mean you are not moving; they signal you have pulled over and stopped. Third, if you have your hazard lights on and you want to signal to turn, you cannot (the lights are both blinking). Fourth, the reflection of the hazard lights off the rain makes it extremely difficult for drivers behind you to see. Think of a strobe light.

Do not turn on your hazard lights in the rain or in fog. Seriously, you may cause an accident and kill someone.

Speaking of laws, just as a warning, it is illegal in many states to have sex in a vehicle. Just an FYI.

Batman Is the Greatest Superhero

This, I realize, may just be the most controversial subject in this book—not immigration, not abortion, not taxes, not gun control, and not religion. But bring up some sort of pop culture and everyone is interested and often vocal. (Note to all: We should be just as vocal on the other subjects, as well. If we were, our leaders might listen.) Anyway, let's get back to this. Batman is the greatest superhero. The easiest way to prove this is with something I saw on the Internet. As we all know, if it is on the Internet, it must be true.

Okay, here we go, the argument that proves Batman is the greatest superhero:

The Hulk with anger management counseling is just a regular guy.

** A list of all fifty states' laws regarding the use of hazard lights is located in the Appendix.

Superman without the Sun is just a regular guy.
Ironman without money and his suit is just a regular guy.
Batman without money is a guy who knows Karate/how to fight.
A guy who knows Karate can beat up just a regular guy.
Case Closed.

American Holidays

There are actually no national holidays in the United States. Congress and the President can legally designate holidays for federal government employees. Each of the fifty states has jurisdiction over its holidays. However, most states observe the federal holidays.

Affect/Effect

Affect is usually a verb, meaning "to have influence upon," such as in "The cost of raising a child did not *affect* my decision to have one."

Effect is usually a noun, such as in "When my lovely wife cooked dinner, the *effect* was the house filled with smoke," or "The things in your luggage are your personal *effects*," or "special *effects*," or "sound *effects*."

Just remember, you can affect an effect.

When you *affect* something, you have an *effect* on it.
*

LACK OF DISCRETION MAKES
FOR A LOT OF NOISE

There used to be a thing called "discretion in the streets." It was considered polite to keep your voice down while in public, to keep your conversations low and limited to the person to whom you are speaking. Believe it or not, it was considered rude to have a conversation while walking on a crowded sidewalk. Often, with the way people practically yell into their cell phones, I wish the old social norms would return and become the norms once again. I suspect I am not the only one who feels this way. Etiquette, manners, social graces—all seem to be lacking in today's "enlightened" society. There are no longer "finishing schools." Why? It is said that George Washington, as a child, practiced his penmanship by copying the passages of the book *Civility & Decent Behavior*. There are 110 passages in that book. While some of the passages may seem outdated, they could be slightly reworded to apply to society today. Perhaps I will have my children copy the passages to practice their penmanship, and perhaps some of the lessons will stick. Perhaps I will copy the passages myself. Maybe even reword them to apply to today's society.

I must point out however one benefit of people's lack of discretion in public; for those in my profession they certainly make it easier to conduct surveillance. Which, as a younger agent I did quite often. ("boots" are usually assigned the grave yard shift. We were also assigned the "dumpster diving", but that is a filthy subject I won't get into.) Too bad I do not do much surveillance anymore. I personally think it would be easier today. (That sounds like an old man, "Back in my day we had to read lips, in the dark, backwards because they were facing a mirror...")

ELECTRONIC LEASHES ARE
DRIVING ME CRAZY

This is not going to be an observation of the unintentional consequences of being connected to everyone, including our jobs, 24/7 via electronic devices, and how these devices have interfered with our personal lives. That subject has been written about and discussed ad nauseam. This is another type of observational exercise.

Take a look around you. Really observe how people behave. In one day, count how many people have their faces buried in their smartphones while in the elevator. Or count how many people are looking at or typing into their smartphones while walking along the sidewalk. Count how many people are on the phone while in the store—not the people who called home to ask their spouse if they need milk, but persons who are having full conversations. Pay attention to how many drivers are obviously using their phones, causing them to drive poorly. After one day of this little exercise, I think you will be amazed. My question is: what is that important? What cannot wait until you have the time to give the person or the issue your full attention? Certainly there is no reason to take a phone call while you are in the restroom, disgusting. Nothing could be that important.

Though, with everyone staring at their phones or tablets out in public, it makes it easier to do a double take of attractive women. They don't notice. Neither does anyone else, for that matter ... except maybe my lovely wife.

CHALLENGE COINS

If you have ever served in the military for a length of time, you have most likely heard of, or perhaps even earned, a challenge coin. Now people in law enforcement and intelligence (myself included) have their own coins; but they started as a military display identification item, which can be traced back to World War II. In that period, a challenge coin was designed and issued to the soldiers who earned them, identifying them as belonging to, or having been a part of, a specific unit. Carrying the coin at all times and presenting it when "challenged" resulted in consequences. The "challenge" usually took place in a bar; therefore, the most popular consequence was for the *challenged* soldier who could not produce a coin to buy the *challenger* a drink. (The misguided notion about the soldier having to buy a round of drinks for those in the entire bar is ridiculous. An enlisted man, then or even now, could not afford to do that without enduring greater consequences, especially if married.)

Although no one really "challenges" anymore, just about everyone is trading. Some people—military, law enforcement, and intelligence—have collections on their desk displaying how many units they have been a part of or, more likely, how many coins they own by trading. It is possible to buy many of these challenge coins, so I would be wary about the guy describing his time fighting in Operation Desert Shield when he looks like he wasn't even old enough to be fighting acne then. Yes, you can buy challenge coins. You can even buy just about every US government agency coin. Two three-letter agencies I used to frequent for work have gift shops. (Yes, they have a gift shop) One has a sign next to the cash register reminding those working undercover not to use their undercover credit cards when making purchases. (I am not making that up.) You can buy challenge coins almost anywhere nowadays. Even restaurants and tourist attractions are now selling challenge coins. Leave it to us to take something that had to be earned and was so special it was almost sacred, and turn it into a trinket collection.

Just terrible... I have about fifty I have traded for. How about you?

LIST OF IMPORTANT PHILOSOPHERS

John Locke
Epicurus
Zeno of Citium
Avicenna
Thomas Aquinas
Confucius
René Descartes
Paul of Tarsus
Plato
Aristotle

**

**Did you think I would just write a list and leave you with nothing more? No explanation? No reason? Well, (that's a deep subject), if you thought that, you must know me. In most cases, you wouldn't be that far off. However, in this case I have decided to include, in the Appendix, a brief summary of each and why I think they are important.

LETTERS ARE ART, WRITING LETTERS IS AN ART FORM

"Do you want to feel insecure? Count the number if Christmas
cards you sent out, and then count those you received."
Milton Berle

"It has been a while since I took pen in hand to write you." I enjoy using that line when writing letters to people with whom I have not spoken in a while. Letters are the perfect way to reconnect with those of whom we have lost contact. I consider letters a form of art. The art of letter writing—selecting the paper to use, perhaps some stationery from a hotel in another country, and then choosing the stamps to place on the envelopes—this is something I enjoy. Although many recipients of my letters might not have noticed, I pay close attention to the stamps affixed to letters. I especially enjoy using older stamps, with the required additional postage to ensure delivery. I think the metrical line of stamps on the front of an envelope that equals forty-six cents (the current price to mail a first-class letter weighing one ounce) looks pretty cool. Add an additional twenty cents if the letter cannot be processed by the postal machines. (Anything that can be caught by the postal machines and needs to be hand sorted, such as wax seals or string ties, costs the additional twenty cents right now.). To me, it adds a bit of history or mystery, at the very least, something different to look at besides your standard addressor and addressee. Yes, even the envelopes can be aesthetically pleasing: art. (In case you were wondering about the weight of letters, yes, I do have a scale on my writing desk, and yes, I do have a special writing desk.)

As I stated before, I consider letter writing an art form. My desk is my studio, sometimes my confessional. Whenever I sit down to pen a letter, it is because I want to share something with a friend. (Side note: I consider everyone close to me a friend. For me, it is a broad term to be used for family, lovers, and of course friends.) Since I want to share something, I want to make the letter as special or unique as possible. I usually include a quote that fits with the overall theme of the correspondence. I like to add a quote to Christmas cards, as well.

Whenever you use a quote, I feel it is important to know something about the person you are quoting. If you don't know off the top of your head, a quick Internet search and a few minutes of reading can rectify that. Why take the time? I personally do not want to be quoting someone with whom I disagree—politically, socially, whatever. Not to mention the fact the friend to whom you are writing may be familiar with the person you are quoting, which could be embarrassing or misrepresent your ideals.

Letters are so much more personal than e-mails or texts. You cannot put an electronic form of communication in a box and go back to it later—unless, of course, you print it. But you cannot imagine the author holding the paper, folding it, and sending it to you. If it was sent by a woman wanting to get a certain point across by spraying it with perfume or leaving a lipstick kiss, the effect is much stronger than an "XO" at the end of a text. When was the last time you held a letter in your hand? When was the last time someone took the time to make sure a letter smelled pleasant for you? Has anyone? It used to be quite common for ladies to spray perfume onto the letters for their boyfriends. I imagine this type of "courting" by our grandparents is one reason we are alive today.

Holding something which was once held by someone else holds a special place for me. This is especially significant when the author is no longer with you. This does not always involve death, but that certainly holds true.

So, letters are art, and writing them is an art form. They are special. There is even another word for a letter: missive. Although, if you were to speak about, "the art of missive writing", you may sound a bit pompous; with which I have no problem. In fact, I often use uncommon words in letters just to make the recipients look them up. That is because I am a jerk, but a good-natured one.

When discussing letters, the US Postal Service and their problems usually come up. When it comes up, someone will usually say something about how no one sends letters anymore and the postal service should be shut down. Don't tell me "no one" sends letters. I guarantee if you received a letter from a friend, it could very well be the highlight of your day. Also, the fact it only costs me only forty-six cents to send a letter, card, or invitation anywhere in the United States and have it arrive within five to seven days is pretty amazing.

FYI: The postal service receives no taxpayer money or federal funding. All of their operational costs are covered by the sales of stamps and other shipping products. I bring it up because I am surprised at how many people do not know that.

FROM A POSTCARD I SENT FROM SAN MIGUEL DE ALLENDE, GTO, MEXICO, IN 1998

Drinking a postcard, writing some tequila,
Tequila here is the national drink,
Not beer or margaritas as one may think,
Last night about a quarter after three,
I poured ten of those concoctions into me.

It was late, it was fun, I should have gone to bed,
This morning I awoke with such a head.

So remember this, my friend, before I depart,
Parting may be a pastime, but drinking tequila is an art.

WHITE SMOKE

The 266th pope was chosen this year (2013) after Pope Benedict XVI resigned. He was the first pope to do so in six hundred years. After a two-day conclave, Jorge Mario Bergoglio, the seventy-six-year-old archbishop of Buenos Aires, was chosen to succeed Pope Benedict. This selection marks the first non-European to be elected pope since the Middle Ages, and he is also the first Jesuit to be declared pope. Archbishop Bergoglio has chosen to be called Francis after St. Francis of Assisi.

My lovely wife and I went to Assisi (and many other cities in Italy) on our honeymoon. If you are lucky enough to happen to visit Assisi, there is a surprising find just outside the city. There you will find a cathedral which was built around and over a small wooden chapel. That chapel is the actual chapel used by St. Francis and his followers for prayer and teaching. He lived in the city but "worked" in that chapel. I found it pretty amazing. Of course, there is a large cathedral inside the city walls dedicated to St. Francis, which is the most popular tourist attraction (which we visited also, out of obligation), but this little wooden chapel seemed more spiritual. It apparently is not well-known. The day my lovely wife and I visited, there were few tourists.

THE BEST DOC IN OLD TOWN

"Some patients, though conscious that their condition
is perilous, recover their health through their
contentment with the goodness of the physician."
-Hippocrates

I hate doctors. Actually I hate everything medical. So it makes absolutely no sense I ended up marrying a nurse. Though, in my defense, I did not know she was a nurse when I was checking out her legs, which extended from under her skirt, in a bar on a Friday night, when we met.

Hate, I realize, is a very strong word, so perhaps I should not throw it around in such a cavalier manner. *Despise*. That is better. I despise doctors. Actually I despise everything medical. I am certain you understand my sentiment.

Doc Nemeth (Richard Nemeth, MD) is younger, athletic, altruistic, and to the point, and he has never tried to bullshit me. (When I say "younger" and "athletic," I am viewing him as a contemporary of mine, and I view myself as younger and athletic. Other persons' views may differ, but I do not let them bother me or influence my perspective.)

When I told him I had taken Excedrin with a beer, he responded how I expected a doctor should respond, but he didn't judge me. (At least he didn't let me know if he did.) Having a doctor with an attitude like that makes it easier for a difficult patient like me to be honest, which I understand is important in order to receive proper medical care. Or that is what I have been told, or maybe read. As I stated before, my attitude toward things medical is not exactly an affectionate one, so I have no idea if the whole "honesty is the best policy" is true.

Doc Nemeth will also not—I repeat, *not*—double- or triple-book appointments, which I understand is not the best financial practice for his Practice. Go to another doctor's office, perhaps even yours, and notice the number of people in the waiting room. Better still, if there is a sign-in sheet, be nosy and take a look at the time of other people's appointments. You will be surprised how many people have an appointment at 1:15 p.m. with Dr. Whoever. Doc Nemeth will not do that. In his waiting room there are rarely more than a couple people. Perhaps that is the reason the waiting room is peaceful and quiet. Or maybe it is just the atmosphere is a reflection of his demeanor. The selection of magazines is not bad either—not that you will have time to finish an article, because you will not be left waiting for long. Ah, the professionalism, the service, the treatment. Do not go to his practice, because if you do, everywhere else will be a disappointment. Okay, perhaps that last sentence was a little over the top. But perhaps it will get past the editor, increasing the word count, which may increase the satisfaction you have after reading this. If it doesn't give you satisfaction, it will increase the time you spent reading. This may come in handy if you find yourself in a situation where you must pass the time, such as sitting in another doctor's office, waiting for your appointment. (See how I did that? See how I brought that back, full circle? Wow, for a minute there I wasn't certain I could pull it off, but then a miracle happened, just like the perfect '72 Dolphins season.)

While I consider Doc Nemeth to be the best doctor from whom I have received treatment, I can only compare him to the doctors to whom I have been exposed. I cannot help myself when it comes to being cynical. I am not a "glass half full" or a "glass half empty" person. I am a "why is that glass so small for the price?" type of guy. In my opinion, the only way to receive the best medical care is to be the president or former president of the United States or a member of Congress or the Senate. The rest of us are screwed. But at least there are, I imagine, other altruistic Doc Nemeths out there, if you can find them.

Wouldn't it be nice if our elected officials were exposed to the same medical care and programs they vote for or sign into law? If they had to live within the constraints of their programs, those programs would be much different. They may even be inclined to support market-based systems with very little government intervention—almost like one would see in a republic ... a representative republic. Wouldn't that be nice?

FRANK BRYANT

"That's special," Lieutenant Colonel Frank Bryan would often say. He was able to take those two words and use them in just about every situation. He would say them with a smirk after hearing a trite comment. He would say them mockingly, if deserved. But most important, no matter how he used those words, he would say them with a smile.

During his deployment as an air adviser to the 438th Air Expeditionary Advisor Group in Kabul, Afghanistan, Lieutenant Colonel Frank Bryant, an air force combat fighter pilot, was the ranking member of the nine people killed on April 27, 2011.

Born and raised in Knoxville, Tennessee, with his call sign "Bruiser," Frank reminded me of the line from a Charlie Daniels Band song: "It took half of Dallas County to put one coon boy in jail" (although he would never have done anything requiring jail). He graduated from Karns High School in 1991, where he was a champion wrestler, winning the Tennessee High School state championship in 1991. He continued wrestling throughout his college career, and in 1995 he served as the team captain and was named most valuable player at the US Air Force Academy.

After graduating from the Air Force Academy in 1995 with a bachelor's degree in general engineering, he attended undergraduate pilot training and became a T-37 instructor pilot. He went on to become a decorated F-16 fighter pilot with 3,047 total flying hours, 121 of which were in combat. During his career, Lieutenant Colonel Bryant served at Columbus Air Force Base, Mississippi; Kunsan Air Base, Republic of Korea; Shaw Air Force Base, South Carolina; and Luke Air Force Base, Arizona. He also served as an exchange pilot to the United Arab Emirates.

In addition to his most recent deployment to the Combined Joint Chiefs of Staff Afghanistan-Pakistan Hands Program as an air advisor to the 438th Air Expeditionary Group, he deployed in 2003 in support of Operation Iraqi Freedom. During his career, he earned his jump wings, senior pilot wings, and a master's degree in business administration and management from Touro University. In 2008 he won the 19th Air Force Air-to-Ground Fighter Pilot Instructor of the Year Award and was named the 19th Air Force Top Instructor Pilot, receiving the General William R. Looney III award.

Lieutenant Colonel Bryant was a recipient of the Bronze Star, Purple Heart, Air Force Combat Action Medal, Defense Meritorious Service Medal, Meritorious Service Medal, Air Force Medal; one oak leaf cluster, Air Force Commendation Medal; one oak leaf cluster; the Air Force Achievement Medal, Joint Meritorious Unit Award, Air Force Outstanding Unit valor device and two oak leaf clusters, Combat Readiness Medal, National Defense Medal, Global War on Terrorism Expeditionary Medal, Global War on Terrorism Service Medal, Korean Defense Medal, Afghanistan Campaign Medal, Non-Article 5 NATO Medal, Air Force Overseas Ribbon (short and long), Air Force Expeditionary Service Ribbon with Gold Border; One Oak Leaf Cluster, Air Force Longevity Service, three oak leaf clusters, and Air Force Training Ribbon.

Bruiser in his uniform, with all his ribbons, was quite imposing especially when I thought about the measly two rows of ribbons I earned in the military. But then he would smile and crack a joke, and you would realize behind all those ribbons was a cool dude.

He served in the United Arab Emirates, where he met his future wife, Janice. I also met Frank while serving in the United Arab Emirates. He was a fighter pilot, and I was an attaché. What an odd pairing. After our tours we both returned to the DC area. Frank and Janice attended my lovely wife's and my wedding. A few months later, we attended theirs. They visited us when our first child was born. A year and a half later, we visited them when their child was born.

One evening, while Janice was pregnant with their son Sean, my lovely wife and I went over to their apartment in Arlington. My wife, being a NICU nurse, was giving them lessons and telling them what to expect with the baby. I think Frank was asking more questions than Janice. He was so excited. I was sitting on the couch in the other room watching the Mecum Auto Auction, drinking gin and tonics.

I remember when Frank and Janice brought newborn Sean over to our house on the first Saturday in May 2011. We were hosting our Kentucky Derby party. The Bryants made an appearance, even though Janice was exhausted and young Sean would not be able to stay long. Frank, holding his son, placed a bet. (It was legal. I had the proper permit from the city of Alexandria for the party.) We had a drink, hugs and kisses and well wishes were exchanged by all, and out they went. That is how he rolled. Having three children of my own, I know what an effort it is to make a "quick visit" anywhere. The visit may be quick, but the preparation, loading, traveling, unloading, reloading, traveling, and final unloading aren't.

Frank deployed to Afghanistan about six months later. He was able to come back and visit his new family once. Then he went back to work. Frank Bryant was my friend.

The Air Warrior Courage Foundation (AWCF) established a college fund for Frank's son Sean. If you wish to contribute, you may send checks directly to: Air Warrior Courage Foundation, P.O. Box 877, Silver Springs, MD 20918. Please annotate "Sean Bryant 529 College Fund" on the check.

FRANK SINATRA

For a few moments, let's view the late fifties and sixties through a narrow lens which doesn't allow politicians, soldiers, civil rights marches, draft cards, Woodstock, Cambodia, or Vietnam in the picture. Let us focus the lens on tail-finned cars, men in fedoras, and women in skirts and heels, wearing red lipstick. Cocktail Culture, where two buttoned suits, starched shirts and everything finished with the goal of being able to accomplish it with style, and probably a beverage. Taking all of this into account, the view of your narrowly focused lens may and should fall upon Frank Sinatra. This is not the old, heavier, "New York, New York" Sinatra; this is the slim, swinging music, fun, Chairman of the Board, Rat Pack before and after Bogart's death Sinatra. The only adults at the time who seemed to be having fun, at least on stage. This is compared to the other adults outside the narrow focus of our lens.

Some Facts

He only recorded with a live band. He stated doing otherwise was like "singing with ghosts."

1957 was the time of his concept albums, (A group of songs related to a theme), such as *Come Fly With Me* and *Come Dance With Me*. Before that, singles were the dominant form.

He helped create the process of recording in "stereo," placing microphones in separate places while recording. *A Jolly Christmas* is probably the best Christmas album ever recorded by anybody.

He trained his breathing for singing by holding his breath underwater in a pool.

He created the Reprise record label. The first album was "Ring-a-Ding-Ding." (You can almost hear a difference in his voice; there is excitement in the tracks.)

He was awesome and the essence of cool and style from 1957 through the mid-1960s. This was after his earlier days of being almost worshipped by bobby-soxers.

When he was younger and much thinner, WB made a parody of him in a cartoon: as a skinny rooster, crooning to chickens (ladies), some of whom fainted in excitement.

He was The Chairman of the Board.
He was Old Blue Eyes.
He was The Voice.

His birthday is December 12. I like to take that day off work to celebrate, ending of course at "… a quarter to three …"

A great book, and an easy read, is *The Way You Wear Your Hat*, by Bill Zehne. When it came out, I gave it as a Christmas gift to the men in my family and several friends.

To sum up and to put Sinatra in perspective, a 1959 quote from the editor of *Jazz* magazine, Ralph Gleason, does it best. "It is as certain a truth that Frank Sinatra is the greatest ballad singer of his generation as that Charlie Parker was a musical genius, Frank Lloyd Wright an architectural poet and Joe DiMaggio, hitting a ball, a thing of Classic Beauty."

MICHAEL JACKSON

Born March 27, 1942, Michael Jackson was arguably the most important person of his genre since the Victorian commentator Alfred Barnard. I am, of course, writing about Michael Jackson, the English writer who specialized in writing and reviewing beer and whiskey.

I am not certain if my father-in-law is a fan of his works, particularly his book *The World Guide to Beer*, published in 1977. Perhaps it is something we can talk about the next time he visits. Love of beer is something we share, along with the love of his eldest daughter. However, his affinity for beer far exceeds mine. He used to keep a journal of tasting notes, recording samples of beers from around the world. Yes, from around the world. (A journal of strictly American beers wouldn't be all that interesting, at least not until the microbrewery explosion.) Wow, I just realized how pompous that sounded, especially from a proud American. Well, (that's a deep subject), pompous it is. You can be proud and realistic at the same time. Most American beers are not as good as other country's beers, especially Belgium, in my opinion.

Anyway, back to Michael Jackson. He wrote several books and articles on beer and whiskey, and he even had a television show, *The Beer Hunter*. Talk about falling into the lucky rabbit hole and doing what you love. Though, if you are enjoying this book and you are, say, among about one hundred thousand people who not only enjoy this book but actually buy this book, then I could be one who falls into that lucky rabbit hole, doing what I love—which isn't writing books. Obviously, I am joking. Not about one hundred thousand people buying this book. That is not a joke. Think of the children, my children. One hundred thousand copies at however much the book costs is ... hold on ... wait a second (I'm an agent, not a mathematician) ... a lot.

Okay, once again, back to Michael Jackson. He also released his own line of beer glassware, which is very nice. If you find yourself wondering what to get me for Christmas, I would definitely like for you to purchase another copy of this book.

Michael Jackson was also reportedly a rugby fan, which should make him a hero of my cousin Scott. You see, my cousin Scott also shares a love of beer and whiskey. He is also a great fan of rugby. So much so he is constantly attempting to start an argument with me about which game is better or which athletes are tougher, football players or rugby players. It is almost a pastime of his at Thanksgiving, in between James Bond movies and dinner. Thank goodness for the beer and/or whiskey.

I bet you thought, from the title, that I was going to write about the other Michael Jackson.

THE BEST BOND

First, if you have not read the books by Ian Fleming, you should stop reading this and go read the original Bond books before entering into this discussion. I realize this could have a negative effect on my financial pleasure, but hopefully you have already purchased this book (to my financial pleasure) and are not reading this particular page while browsing at the bookstore. Telling people to stop reading your book and go read another is not the best of advertising strategies, I would imagine. Anyway, back to the topic: the best Bond.

Reading the original books is really the only way to be properly prepared for this debate, unless you are interested in only the movies, with no interest in the actual basis of the character and subject material. If that is the unfortunate case, any real debate will become as shallow as voting for the prom king and queen. That does not mean you cannot have the discussion, but just know you will be discussing pop culture through the eyes of a teenager.

Now that I have probably insulted half the people actually reading this, let me begin. To most people, when you mention James Bond, they think of Sean Connery. Why wouldn't they? Although he was not the first actor to play the role (seriously, there was a TV movie—look it up), he was the first actor to play the part in a major motion picture: *Dr. No*. In that movie, Sean Connery portrayed the character, as described in the book. Except for the ending and a couple other changes to make the movie more exciting on screen, the movie stayed very close to the book. So Connery had excellent material to work with, and he physically resembled the character described in the book and resembled Ian Fleming's commissioned image of James Bond. It is important to know that *Dr. No* was the sixth book in the series; therefore, the character was well established, and this is evident in the movie, as well. You can watch the movie and see all the players are at ease with their surroundings. Not much explanation is necessary.

Also, in the movie, Sean Connery showed the savage nature of the character in the scene in the river, when he kills an adversary without any emotion. After reading the first few books, you get the feeling that Bond is good at his job, because he is a sycophantic, selfish, womanizing, ruthless killer, with a conscience and that ever-present shadow of a doubt. When I mentioned Connery having good material to work with, this is something everyone should take into account when entering into this debate. Any actor can be horrible if the script is horrible, and the same could be said when the opposite is in play.

But back to the best Bond. To me, the movies that closely follow the books make it easier to judge the actor playing the role. When the script has too many corny jokes, it takes away from the serious nature of the character. The books often reveal Bond's inner thoughts, which explain much of how and why he acts a certain way. Timothy Dalton explained some of the inner thoughts of Bond in an interview after he played Bond in the movie *The Living Daylights*. Personally I thought Dalton played the character exactly as Fleming described him, even though the script was not great. The movie left out certain portions from the short story on which it was named and basically made a mess. Still, Dalton managed to show the darker, human aspects of the character.

I think, given a good script, Connery, Dalton, and Pierce Brosnan could play the character, as imagined in the books. While Daniel Craig is a great actor, and the movie *Casino Royal* had a good script, Craig does not look like the character described in the original books.

You may have noticed I have not mentioned Lazenby or Moore. The movie *On Her Majesty's Secret Service* followed the book pretty closely except for some corny jokes and other scenes. It also broke a movie rule when, in the first scene, it acknowledged it was a movie and another actor had played the role—a terrible decision, in my mind, and it almost ruined the movie for me. George Lazenby looked the part but didn't play it. You could blame it on the script, but as I mentioned, parts of the script followed the book exactly. Lazenby just didn't nail it. It would have been interesting to see Connery in that movie. He could have pulled off wearing a kilt, being a Scotsman and the script as I mentioned was much better than the next film. Unfortunately he passed on it only to return in the next Bond picture *Diamonds are Forever.*

Now to Roger Moore, the actor who played the part in the most movies. The movies were popular, which is why they kept making them, but they didn't have the seriousness of the books. If the scripts had been different, who knows if Moore could have played the role? I personally do not think so; to me, he didn't fit the character, as described in the books. However, the movies in which he starred are enjoyable for what they are. I would describe them as "popcorn movies."

I realize I keep mentioning the books, but that is because they are so enjoyable and easy to read, as hours were spent in intimate contact with the characters and with the author. Before I read all the books, I read a biography of Ian Fleming, *Ian Fleming: The Man Behind James Bond*, by Andrew Lycett. The biography is terrific. Once you get through his family history, his life and experiences are just as thrilling as his books. If you read the biography before reading the books, you can also see how he incorporates his experiences into the stories. Becoming a fan of a book—or, in this case, a series of books—is a thrilling experience. If you decide to read the books, I suggest reading them in order. Occasionally the stories flow together, but more important, you can see the character develop over the course of the books.

Okay, back to the best Bond. As you can see, I am not exactly being fair by comparing the books to the movies. You should actually think of them as two separate forms of entertainment. The movies have a sort of disclaimer when the opening credits roll; they state, "_____ as Ian Fleming's James Bond." So if you take the subjects and separate them— James Bond the movie, and James Bond the book—you could have two answers. But since this is my essay, I am not going to separate them. James Bond in the books, who do you picture in your mind's eye while reading? Fleming was pretty deliberate in his description and in the image of the character he commissioned to aid the *Daily Express* comic strip artists.

(Yes, there was a James Bond comic strip.) Who is the best Bond? Barry Nelson, David Niven, Connery, Lazenby, Moore, Dalton, Brosnan? For me, I have narrowed it down to three actors who have played the part: Sean Connery, Timothy Dalton, and Pierce Brosnan. All three of them physically look like the character described in the books. The movie scripts allowed each of them to display at least one of the personality traits or emotions from the books, be it the savage side or the melancholy side or the dynamic side. Yes, I wrote dynamic. You would certainly feel his presence if the character were to walk into a room simply based on his experiences. As Fleming stated about his character, "Exotic things would happen around him, but he would be a neutral figure – an anonymous, blunt instrument wielded by a government department."

So, who is the best?

FERAL CATS, OR NEIGHBORHOOD CAT LADY

There is a couple who lives in our neighborhood and feeds feral cats. These are not stray cats, but feral cats. (There is a difference. You can look it up.) So these critters are not simply homeless, little, lovable, furry creatures, but they are fully grown, disease-carrying, small dog-killing, dangerous, annoying, and reproducing feral cats. We did not realize this situation when my lovely wife and I decided to buy our house and move our family into the neighborhood. (Actually, there are several things about the neighborhood we didn't realize, but let's just stick to the cat situation for now.) One morning when I went out to retrieve the paper, I realized these things were going to be more than a little nuisance, when I discovered feces in my yard, where my children like to play.

So, being the reasonable, normal person I am, I did the reasonable, normal thing, which was to ask the couple not to feed the cats. Their response was "You cannot starve them away." which I researched and discovered, unfortunately, to be true. Being the reasonable, normal person, I replied, "If you feel so strongly about feeding the feral cats, would you limit the feeding to just your yard?" (Oh, did I mention they leave food for the little carriers of toxins all around the neighborhood?) Well, (that is a deep subject), as you may guess from the fact there is more to read, they declined.

Facing the situation sagaciously, I did what any reasonable, normal person would do; I went out and bought a high-powered BB gun. I thought it was a pretty good idea until my lovely wife informed me it was illegal—not to purchase the BB gun, but to proceed with my sagacious and reasonable plans. So, being a law-abiding citizen, I ceased with my BB gun plans. (I just wish I knew who was lighting what sounds like a firecracker near my home every so often … when there happens to be a cat around.)

Something to think about: The cost of a rabies vaccine is very high and fluctuates depending upon where you live. The treatment involves getting a series of shots, which means several trips to the hospital, doctor's office, or clinic. The first shot is the human rabies immunoglobulin (HRIG), and this shot alone costs several thousand dollars. Yes, thousands. Feral cats carry rabies, among other things.

THE ART OF PERSUASION

"Sincerity is everything. If you can fake that, you've got it made."
—George Burns

Here I go again, describing something as an art form. But I think it is true. In fact, I agree with the description of many things called art—martial arts, for example. Of course it can be violent, but it is still art. Though I do not consider a crucifix in a jar (you know the rest) art. I consider that distasteful.

The art of persuasion, for the life of me—where did that phrase "for the life of me" come from? What does it really mean? Does it mean "Kill me, because I do not know"? Ah, these clichés ... I will address them later. For now, keep reading. That's it, just like you are now. Very good. See how easy this is?

Where was I? Persuasion. I cannot remember where I learned all of the following. I do know the original thoughts are not all my own; rather, they are things I picked up or learned over the past twenty years of my profession. Some I learned in boot camp, some in the academy, some in add-on classes, some from partners and mentors, some from criminals, and others from just reading. Therefore, I submit the following as knowledge I have learned from others and would like to pass along to you now.

It is important to note none of these methods fall under what I would term the "dark arts of influencing people." Anything that could be harmful, especially to someone's self-esteem, is not included here. There are ways to win friends and ways to influence people using psychology and observation without making someone feel bad. There are enough people out there who naturally have that ability to make others feel bad; we do not need any more of them.

Be a Good Listener

This is a given. People like to hear themselves speak. People especially like to speak when they know the person they are talking to is actually listening. So, listen. Actively listen. Let them tell you all they have to say about whatever it is they are speaking about. Don't just pretend to listen while actually thinking about what you want to say when they stop speaking. Listen. Ask a few follow-up questions. When they are finished, they might even feel obliged to listen to you. Go ahead and take it from there.

Ask for Favors

This is known as the Benjamin Franklin effect. You can easily find this example on the Internet, but I am thankful you have decided to read about it in this book. It breaks down to this: Ask someone who does not like you to do something for you. For some physiological reason, that person will no longer have the same negative feeling for you. Part of it, I suppose, has to do with the fact when you ask someone for a favor, you are acknowledging to a person that you need that person's help, and that person is superior to you in a way. People like to feel powerful, and this feeds an ego. The other part of the theory is if someone does a favor for you, that person rationalizes subconsciously you must be worth doing a favor for. If you are worth doing a favor for, you must not be all that bad.

Benjamin Franklin said, "He that has once done you a kindness will be more ready to do you another, than he whom you yourself have obliged."

In *Franklin: Writings*, he explained how he dealt with a rival legislator.

> Having heard that he had in his library a certain scarce book, I wrote a note to him, expressing my desire of perusing that book, and requesting he would do me the favor of lending it to me for a few days. He sent it immediately, and I returned it in about a week with another note, expressing strongly my sense of the favor.

When we next met in the House, he spoke to me (which he had never done before), and with great civility; and he ever after manifested a readiness to serve me on all occasions, so that we became great friends, and our friendship continued to his death.

I personally have used this technique while working undercover. Getting my target to do me a favor almost immediately made me trustworthy, allowing me to infiltrate, in one particular case, the organization more quickly and successfully than originally hoped. That, however, is something I may write about at another time.

Selling a Car Technique

Ask for more than you are trying to acquire, giving yourself room and the appearance you are negotiating fairly. This is hardly news to anyone who is able to purchase (hopefully you purchased) this book and has read up to this page, but it is still worth stating. I would imagine you have done this several times in your life, if you have had a garage sale, sold a car, or in today's world, placed something for sale on eBay or Craigslist.

What's in a Name?

In *How to Win Friends and Influence People,* Dale Carnegie wrote that using someone's name is extremely important. According to him, a person's name is the sweetest sound in any language for that particular person. Our name is the central part of our identity, and hearing our name validates our existence. Hearing our name being uttered by someone makes us have positive feelings about the person who "validated" us.

Using a nickname can also have similar effects. If you act like a certain type of person, you will become that person. To use this in the art of persuasion, you can refer to someone as you want them to be. By doing this, they will begin to think of themselves this way. If those two sentences seemed confusing, let me explain it in a different way. With something as simple as calling an acquaintance by a more intimate nickname, this will over time have an effect on how that person feels about you. Whenever you see the person, refer to him as "mate" or "buddy." For the opposite sex, refer to her as "darling." Over time, they will begin to think of themselves as this to you. (Word of caution: if you refer to someone you are trying to influence as "boss," and they just happen to be your boss, you sound like a tool to everyone who hears you, including your boss.)

Conclusion

The easiest and best way to persuade someone is to simply be nice and not ask for anything too outrageous. (But if I had just written that, it would have significantly reduced the word count of this book.)

LYING, PARTIAL TRUTHS, AND OFFICIAL STATEMENTS

"If George Washington never told a lie,
how did he become President?"
-Milton Berle

You cannot run away from who you are any more than you can run away from the truth. But it is how you hide the truth that counts. Now, I am not justifying lying, but not everyone needs to know everything. This is certainly true when certain types of statements are made.

All the information you receive is a lie in one way or another. I write that statement with confidence, because to me, an omission of fact is lying or at least knavery. This is often necessary. You may notice I am not writing this in a negative tone ... yet.

Everyone is a liar (it is just like I told the judge), but which liar are you going to believe? Now that is the question you should be asking.

Every lie has 80 percent truth to it. (Don't ask me how I know or came to that last statement. I made it up. That is not a lie.)

Perhaps I am being too harsh, and perhaps, just perhaps I am being too cynical. Twenty years of government service may have something to do with it. Or maybe I am just naturally hostile. If I sound like an angry old man, it is my experiences which have made me that way. (And I am not old, just older.) Regardless, there will come a time when you need to know whom you are going to trust. Now with all this lying I have been mentioning, you are most likely wondering how in the world you will be able to trust anyone. A simple and yet cynical way to determine if you can trust someone is to ask two important questions: (1) What do I want? (2)

Does the person in question want what I want, or will this person benefit in any way from me getting what I want?

If they benefit, I trust them.

Official Statements

Oh my. Exactly why do we, as a nation, continue to listen to leaders even after they receive four "Pinocchios"* after a speech? Why do we listen to the numbers they throw at us? For example: "This bill will create nine hundred thousand jobs," or "Blah blah blah, 25 percent increase in net worth for one billion people." That sort of thing. You can't actually believe some staffer researched, analyzed, and came to those figures with any sort of solid formula or calculations behind it. Well, (deep subject), I cannot. It seems to me we, the public, and they, the public servants, have become numb to numbers, especially large numbers. How could we not, with the current national debt in the trillions of dollars? Most of us cannot really wrap our minds around figures like that. How many zeros is that? No, really, I'm asking. I'm an agent, not a mathematician. Speaking of larger numbers, did you know the tax law is now more than seventy thousand pages long? (That is not a lie or a partial truth.)

Now there are certain statements one should never lie when making. Those include: wedding vows, oaths of office, and promises to children.

I have a terrific conclusion to this essay—which will have to wait. I need to go. There is something really important that needs to be taken care of right away... I could be lying.

---

* The Fact Checker website rates "the truth behind the rhetoric". A "Pinocchio" is given for each exaggerated statement.

MAKE IT HAPPEN

"The greatest way to live with honor in this
world is to be what we pretend to be."
—Socrates

Now I am not certain if the majority of people actually concern themselves with honor on a daily basis anymore. Meaning, when they wake up in the morning, honor may not be the first thing they think of. I would like to think at some point in the day honor or performing honorably comes to mind for most people. Especially persons in professions where honor and integrity are expected, or in positions where an oath is required to be taken. Most of the people I know fall into these categories which is easily explained by the path my life has taken. But that is not what I am going to write about now. The quote by Socrates has a different meaning or lesson in it. For me, it means if you want to be somebody, be it. Like the saying from the eighties, "to be the man, you gotta be the man." For instance, if you want to have a family that eats meals together and has perfect table manners, then be the family that eats meals together, and instruct your children (and spouse, if necessary) proper table manners. Then after time and much patience, you will gaze upon your family eating dinner together in harmony. Of course it may not be until your children are visiting from college when proper table etiquette sets in, but the whole harmony thing is something to strive for.

Hopefully you can see that it is not all too difficult. Okay, perhaps the family eating together was a poor example. The glorious thing about writing is you can always change or start again. So back to the quote, "…to be what we pretend to be." Be careful. You can pretend to be rich, which is fine until you are crying at the check. You can pretend to be righteous, which is fine until you are asked to stand up.

THAT'S SO CLICHÉ

Isn't it funny that, if you respond, "That's so cliché," to someone who used a cliché, you are using a cliché? As promised, I am now addressing the subject of clichés. If you just happened to have opened the book to this essay, the previous sentence won't make any sense to you. If that is the case, you have two options. You could continue reading this particular essay, which is so enthralling you are actually reading the next word and this word and this one too, or you could go back and read every previous essay until you find the reference that makes the second sentence make sense.

The choices are kind of like shaving a mustache. If you are a guy who has ever had a mustache (or a woman—I am not judging here), the following example will make sense. You are shaving, and you accidentally shave too far on one side. You know if you were to shave the other side the same way, it would look ridiculous, like Hitler. So you go ahead and completely shave one side to see how you look without a mustache, because it has been a while since you have seen yourself clean shaven. Then, as you look into the mirror, you realize your options: you can shave the other side, or you can wait until the shaved side grows back.

The options for finding out the explanation for the second sentence in this essay are pretty much the same thing. Now, if you have already read the essay in which I promised to address the subject of clichés later, the examples above were a complete waste of your time, unless you are in a waiting room in the office of a doctor other than Doc Nemeth. (If the doctor's office reference does not make sense to you, it is because you did not read the essay in which I referenced it. If that is the case, you have two choices... Don't worry, I am not going to put you through the options again.)

Seriously, if you have been patiently reading, waiting for me to address the subject of clichés, I apologize for the wait.

Many, if not most, of the clichés we use in our everyday conversation come from the writings of Shakespeare and Benjamin Franklin. If you are like me and enjoy Shakespeare, you have recognized this. If you are like a lot of people (meaning not like me), you were turned off by Shakespeare because your ninth-grade English-Lit teacher was awful and probably in a union. (If you are in a union, I was only kidding. If you are an awful ninth-grade English-Lit teacher, I am not.).

There are many reasons people use clichés in both conversation and writing. They are used in the same way people use quotes, which was addressed in a previous essay. If you haven't read … (only kidding). Clichés, like quotes, can be used to fill in the blanks or to make us sound intelligent, or at least interesting to persons of the opposite sex—that is, if you are in your twenties and single and in a bar on a Friday night, where twenty-somethings should be, trying to seem interesting or appealing to persons of the opposite sex and not on some website looking to seem interesting. Seriously, go out and live. Don't just sit home and read about it—unless, of course, you are reading this book, which you hopefully purchased, making it a financial pleasure to me and a comfort to you, because he/she wasn't the right one for you anyway, so just stay home this Friday and get your head straight before heading back out. (Did you catch the cliché?)

So to address clichés, there is no address if you wanted to send a letter. However, you can look it up in the Appendix of this book. In fact, there is an alphabetical list of many popular clichés in the appendix. The list, unfortunately, is not all-encompassing, but should you ever need an index for clichés, having this book is better than looking for a needle in a haystack.

SMALL TALK, OR USELESS CONVERSATION (OR IS IT)

Small talk. I am not a particular fan of small talk. Unfortunately, for many professions, including mine, small talk is practically a requirement; that and report writing. While it can be painful, especially when the person with whom you are engaging would only be interesting as a tree and you were a male dog, there are things you can do to make it easier for yourself, thus limiting your urge to urinate and containing the damage caused by the potential mental brow beating. The first thing to remember is it may not be a complete waste of time. In my profession, I have used small talk to gain all sorts of information and insight into people, their lives, and their mental prowess. But that is for another day.

Just as in other aspects of life, being prepared is important. Arm yourself. Arm yourself in a way that you can make the following statement and it won't be boasting: "I would challenge you mentally, but frankly you are unarmed." You must be well informed or more to the point well read. I cannot stress enough how important it is and how fulfilling it is to read the newspaper. Some will say they get all the news they need from the Internet or cable news. Indeed, they are receiving some information, but they are only getting the information they seek out. Follow me here. If you are seeking news on the Internet, you are only reading what you want, most likely from sites which share your point of view. You must realize this is a limited way to 'arm' yourself with information. One of the great things about reading the newspaper is you never know what you may come across, be it articles, advertisements, or announcements, and you do not need to read the entire thing. You can still read what interests you. As you come across different articles, what interests you may surprise you. Just glancing at the headlines and titles of articles can be useful. You can say, "Oh, yes, I saw an article on that in the *Wall Street Journal* the other day." Notice I did not say "read." I said "saw." But the person you are talking to heard that you are informed about the topic he/she mentioned. That person is also probably thinking, *Wow, you read the* Wall Street Journal *every day.*

Also arm yourself with current events. Current events and the weather are clichéd things to talk about, but they are clichéd for a reason. They work. Sports are other topics that are easy to talk a lot about with very little knowledge. If you do not want to be confrontational or have your personal beliefs end up as public knowledge, try to stay away from politics. Religion is a given.

Try not to bounce from one topic to another too quickly. If you do, you could find yourself out of 'ammunition' and end up 'unarmed'. Pace yourself. Just as in music and sex, tempo is everything.

NO, I CAN'T

"When a fellow says, 'It ain't the money but the
principle of the thing', it's the money."
Ebert Hubbard

Honor and sincerity are the qualities I admire and expect from my friends. Just be honest with me. That is my first rule of friendship. (The second rule often involves photo negatives and a payment plan, but that is for another time.) Be honest. "I could have helped, but I just didn't want to." Why is it people are afraid to say "no"? What is wrong with a simple no? Not an exaggeration or an elaborate excuse. Just a simple, "No, I can't." Answering, "No, I don't want to" may be closer to the truth, but "No, I can't" seems like it should work just fine.

Anything is better than having someone say they will help you, even reluctantly, and then they don't. Perhaps this is why I rarely ask people for help. If I do, I usually offer to pay them, which I have been told may run the risk of belittling the relationship. But if I would pay a stranger, I figure, why not?

Just recently, I was lied to by someone who told me he would help but then did not. Not only did he not help, but he disappeared for an entire weekend when I tried to reach him.

There is absolutely nothing wrong with, in my opinion, telling people no if they ask for assistance. If honesty is the best policy, then be honest. Let the world know you are not as generous as they think you are or think you should be. And if you are asking, no, I do not want to help you move into your new apartment this weekend.

ADD

I don't believe it. I just don't, and I know writing this will cause many of you to stop reading. If you are in a bookstore and just happened to have opened to this page because the title seemed interesting, but you disagree with the first two sentences of this essay, that goes against the purpose of this book—which, as I have written in other essays contained herein, is to hopefully put at least one of my children through college. In other words, be a financial pleasure.

I don't believe it even though my Goddaughter was diagnosed with it. Doctors often can be and often are wrong. I don't believe the research. I don't believe the articles about it. (Just because it is in print doesn't make it true.) I don't believe the commercials. And I don't believe the children. (Children lie. Don't believe me? Have one, and get back to me when they start talking.)

If it is true, and A.D.D. is an actual disorder, then I have the opposite. I have attention overload disorder. It is both a blessing and a curse. The fact I can listen to multiple conversations at once has served me well (that's a deep subject) in my profession throughout the years. However, hearing everything also makes it difficult to rest in public. You may be thinking, *Who rests in public?* Well, (deep) how about on an airplane? Or the beach? Wait, the surf drowns out most noises, (ha, "surf," "drown"), much like white noise. (I had a white noise generator outside the door to my office in DC so people couldn't listen in on conversations or phone calls. And that office was inside a secure suite. Ah, the world of classification and clearances. It is much different from what it seems on the outside to those who do not work in the environment. Much like Catholicism, if you don't practice it, you really don't understand it.) Now where was I? Ah, yes, the beach. Anyway, it is a curse. (Not the beach.)

I have suggested the following test throughout the years, changing the mechanism as the children age and the technology changes, to prove my point that A.D.D does not exist. If the child can sit and play a video game for hours at a time, or sit in front of the computer for hours on end, or focus on anything for a long period of time, they do not have A.D.D. They just want to do what they like to do. To put it another way, they are acting like children.

Young boys are more aggressive and active and seem to have more energy than their female counterparts, at least in my experience. They don't want to do math. They want to go outside and play soldiers or cowboys and Indians. That is normal. We don't need to medicate them so they will sit still and be quiet in the classroom. Doesn't that sound like "doping" to anyone else? Give anyone medication to calm them down, and they will calm down. That does not necessarily mean they are more focused or even retaining what is being taught. To my knowledge, (and I recently looked this up), there is no study that proves children on A.D.D. medication do any better or have less rates of repeating grades than those children who are not medicated.

It is a fact about which many will disagree with me. My dear friends and parents of my Goddaughter disagree with me. Okay, I am not judging anyone who has made a decision when it comes to trying to help their children. First, it is not my place. Second, I have children of my own and will do all I can to help, not harm, them. Also, I am not suggesting giving children these types of medication doesn't make the children easier to control, but isn't that what parenting is? Doping them seems like a lazy way out to me. If this seems harsh or out of touch or even ignorant, I cannot help it.

Some other thoughts ...

- Medication isn't always the answer.
- Pharmaceutical companies are businesses at their core. The purpose of a business is to make money.

- I think some doctors are making money with quick, easy fixes that some parents are buying, hook, line, and sinker.

One last thought ...

Just because it is in print doesn't make it true. Don't believe everything you read ... perhaps even this.

WHAT IF I FALL?

I asked that question of my Granddaddy when he and I climbed up onto a tree stand on his farm one summer when I was a boy of about seven years old. This tree stand was not the modern type you see in Bass Pro Shops or in catalogs. This was two-by-fours nailed into the tree up to a piece of plywood overlooking a field tree stand. Just climbing up was an adventure for me. No ladder, just pieces of wood nailed into the tree. My Granddaddy had several of these types of tree stands around the many fields of his farm. They were used to kill the deer that ate his crops. Don't cringe at the word "kill." I could have said hunt, but as my Granddaddy told me, sitting in a tree stand and shooting is not hunting. Hunting involved being on the ground, using dogs, and it usually involved a lot of running.

My Granddaddy was old school. If you killed an animal, you ate it. There was no sport hunting on his property. That was the way I was taught. Venison is actually quite tasty if prepared properly. I bring this up just to make the point that the tree stands were for a purpose and not for sport.

"What if I fall?" was the question I asked on this particular morning. My Granddaddy and I had climbed up to the tree stand, and he had given me a pair of binoculars. My "job" that morning was to observe what was going on in and around the field. He was going to plow another field that morning, so looking back on it, this was just giving a seven-year-old boy something to do for a couple hours to keep him out of trouble. When I asked the question, he looked at me with disbelief in his eyes and a hint of sympathy. (I only spent a couple months a year at the farm, so he referred to me as a "city slicker" and always said that by the time my common sense came back, it was time for me to leave.) He told me that I wouldn't fall, but his firm, nurturing nature came through, so he told me he was going to teach me how to tie a slipknot. He said he would tie a cord around my wrist and to the tree, and that should be enough. When I say "enough," it was enough to ease the apprehensions of a seven-year-old. It obviously wasn't enough to keep me from falling out of the tree stand. The cord was thicker than string but thinner than rope. (He always seemed to have a spool of cord and a pocketknife on hand.) So he showed me how to tie it and then tied it for me. He also left me a piece of cord and told me to practice if I was tired of looking through the binoculars.

Today's society may judge the actions of my grandparent as negligent and dangerous. To me that is a shame. So there I was, "safely" tied to the tree, on the tree stand with my binoculars and a piece of cord to practice tying knots, which is where I was to stay for an hour or so while my Granddaddy went to plow another field. I didn't ask for a snack, because we had just eaten breakfast. I didn't ask for something to drink, because I wasn't going to be there long. Can you imagine that happening today? I can't. Not even with my own children. I have become just as "soft" with them as the rest of society. It seems even I have forgotten that our children are not as fragile as we treat them. It is not their fault they need to have everything right in front of them at any given time. It is our fault. We are failing to teach our children how life really works and the difference between needs and wants.

I learned so much on that farm about life, death, and living. Lessons that unfortunately, my own children will never be able to experience or learn the way I did. When you see an animal being born and then you help raise it, feed it, and then you learn how to butcher it for food, you understand how life works. This may seem cruel to some people who never think of how or where their dinner came from. On that farm we planted vegetables and fruit. As I got older, I realized why we "visited" our grandparents in the summer. It was harvest time; we were there to work. To this day I do not like squash. I don't like it because I hated picking it. Their vines had tiny little spikes, and you had to reach into it to get to the fruit. I had to pick it, but by goodness I wasn't going to eat it. (This was when I was older. When I was little I had to eat what I was given. There were no short-order cooks to satisfy the cravings of a pouty four-year-old.)

I wish all children, including my own, could learn the life lessons they will need for a successful future. Now I am not advocating leaving your child up in a tree for a couple hours. (You may go to prison for that now.) But I am suggesting letting your children know that they do not always need a bottle of water beside them. They do not need a bag of food at the ready at all times. What even happened to "If you had eaten your dinner, you wouldn't be hungry." Our world is not an easy place. It is not too difficult, but you must be prepared. Competition is everywhere—for a job, for a seat at the table, and for a mate or companion. Things are not just given to you because you want them. This is the problem I see with the youth today. I even see it in my profession. The new agents expect rank and praise immediately, without doing anything. They feel it is owed to them for just being there.

"What if I fall?" That isn't exactly the question my daughter asked me the other day, but it was close, close enough to make me remember my Granddaddy. My four-year-old daughter wanted a fishing pole. She must have seen one on the Disney Channel in a cartoon. (By the way, if you are a parent or are going to become a parent, come to terms with the fact that Disney owns you! They own you until your children hit puberty. Just deal with it. I did by buying stock.) So I bought my daughter and her almost-three-year-old sister fishing poles. (Oh, yes, I bought one for each. Again, if you are a parent or are going to become one to siblings close in age, just buy two. Avoid the fights. Spend the money, and have some peace.)

I took my daughter out to the dock near our home with her new fishing pole and sat down, letting my legs hang over the edge. I told my daughter to sit beside me so I could show her how to cast. This was when she said, "But, Daddy, I do not want to fall over the edge. You have to hold me." So I told her to go ahead and sit beside me, I wouldn't let her fall, and I would show her something before teaching her how to use her new fishing pole. I took out a spool of cord from my tackle box, tied one edge to the cleat beside us, and said, "Let me show you a slipknot."

RUNNING AROUND

This is not an essay about infidelity. I am Catholic, so that activity is frowned upon. This is about actual running. (Don't worry, you did not accidently fall into an issue of *Men's Health* or *Running*. I am not going to write about anything technical.) Those who know me know I love to run. (Those who knew me, knew I loved to run around ... but that was before I met the lovely lady who eventually became my wife.) Back to running. I have been fortunate to travel quite extensively over the past twenty years. In fact, I have been able to run in several countries on five of the seven continents.

Like most people who run, I have my favorite routes depending upon how far I would like to go and where I want to run. I will list some of my favorite places and routes to run below. Most of them are seven to ten miles, but the great part is all of them are either a complete circle or are a "there and back" route, meaning you can shorten or lengthen them depending upon your mood, your fitness level, and in many cases the weather. Enjoy, but remember the more stressed out you are, the faster you run (at least for me).

San Francisco

There is a public parking lot located off Marina Boulevard, just before the Yacht Club. A lot of people park there to access the Marina Green, which is a large grassy area right beside the bay. Anyway, I like to park there and have never had a problem finding a spot.

Start there and head toward the Golden Gate Bridge. Don't take the easy route and head for Fort Point below the bridge. When you reach the section of the running/biking route that goes toward the right, cross the street, and head left up that hill to the bridge. The traffic is used to pedestrians and bikers. Once you reach the beginning of the Golden Gate Bridge, cross it, touch the sign at the end of the bridge on the other side, and run back. If you do this run and jump up to touch that green sign, tell me what it is made of. (You can e-mail me at: ajumbleofthoughts@ writeme.com) I know there will be tourists and bikers to deal with, but the run is worth it. Keep in mind, on a sunny day, there can be sleet in the middle of the bridge, seriously.

This is one of my favorite runs, and I always try to do it when I am in the area. After the run, you can drive or walk to the Safeway to buy Gatorade. It is located right around the corner from where you parked. I have a great story about doing exactly that after a run with a friend of mine. But I will save that story about Chris and a Supermodel for another time.

London

I used to like to stay at the Green Park Hilton in London for two reasons. There was a casino right around the corner, and it was right on Green Park, which is within walking distance to a couple of my favorite spots. To give you an idea of the location, if you were to run/walk directly across Green Park from the hotel you would be at Buckingham Palace. For the run, you exit right out of the hotel and head toward Green Park. Once there you can run around the park or through it. You can also run to Notting Hill from the hotel and walk through the market on Saturday mornings, but if the market is your sort of thing, I suggest you take a taxi.

Washington, DC

I have lived "near the flag pole" on three different occasions in my career. During these times I have found several different routes to run, and the people I ran/worked with gave each of these names. I will list three here:

"Bridge," "Point," and "Boathouse." Each one has different scenery and is a different distance.

You want to run boathouse when the weather is sunny and warm, during the late spring or summer, because the interns and college students go out to sunbathe on the grass by the Potomac during their lunch breaks. (Just don't trip on a tree root that has broken through the sidewalk. It's easy to miss if you are ogling a hottie as you run by ...)

Sydney

From the Hyde Park Sheraton (Sheraton on the Park), cross the street, run through Hyde Park, continue up Macquarie Street, and stay just to the left of the Royal Botanic Gardens. If you do this you will end up at the Sydney Opera House. (If you accidently go deep into the Botanic Gardens, you can make it to the Opera House, but it will be a much longer run as you wind your way through the park.)

If you want to stay with bridge runs, the Hanger Bridge or Sydney Harbour Bridge is another to add to your list. You can start at Foundation Park and go from there. Just be warned, there seems to be more tourists than on the Golden Gate Bridge.

Paris

I love Paris. I really do, and I have been there quite a few times. Unlike some of the portrayals of people in the media, I do not find the citizens rude at all. The women are gorgeous, which is a great thing when you are sitting in an outdoor café, drinking wine, and enjoying the view. The only negatives are the airport (I think Charles De Gaulle Airport is the worst airport anywhere, and I have been all over the world, including the Middle East, during war.) and the traffic. Other than that, I love Paris.

When I go to Paris, I like to stay at the Sofitel Paris Le Faubourg Hotel. It is right across from the Buddha Bar and right around the corner from the US Embassy. (As you now may have guessed, my visits to Paris were mostly work-related.)

Okay as for the run, go right out of the hotel and up to the US Embassy, and turn right onto Avenue Gabriel. Across the street is a park. You can run through the park or around it. It is a terrific run, and when you are finished you can grab a well-deserved beer at a small café inside the park near the start of the run.

By the way, if you start the same way but turn right onto Avenue Gabriel, across the street is another park that leads up to the Louvre Museum. There are small cafés in that park, as well.

Fort Lauderdale

This is a great city with a lot of cultural events, when the weather is good. I mention the weather because you do not want to visit in the rainy season or the hurricane season.

All right, start at the New River Hotel, which is located right on Las Olas Boulevard. (If you stay there, you are right in the middle of everything and just a couple miles from Fort Lauderdale Beach, which you can run to, which is what I am writing about.) Turn right out of the hotel, and run on the sidewalk (try to avoid this during lunch hour) all the way to the beach, crossing the Intercoastal on the way. Once you are at the beach, you can turn left and run up the strip, people watching along the way, or you can head back to the hotel.

After you are finished and cleaned up, you will not need to get into a car to go to dinner. Everything is right outside the door.

IT NEVER ENDS

The way certain people behave with regards to cliques and how they treat people never ends. You could say High school never ends. It is important to let your children know this. If they happen to be the unlucky ones who are having a hard time with bullies or cliques, you should let them know there will be people who delight in that sort of behavior throughout their lives. I did not have those issues in high school. I had a blast. My lovely wife was on the other side; the first part of her high school career was spent in Europe and the other half in the States. The transition back to the States wasn't easy for her. As you age and move through life you will find the same issues and the same people in the workplace. Their insouciance towards others can at time be quite cruel. This is why, in my opinion, it is important to prepare your children for the future. As much as I would like to, it will be of no benefit to my children for me to fight their battles. Unfortunately, they need to learn how to fend for themselves—with parental guidance, of course. It is our responsibility as parents to arm our children with the knowledge and skills necessary for them to lead productive lives and be positive members of society. Yes, as I have written before, we will be leaving society for them to run, so we had better give our input now, making certain we, the parents, provide the guidance, not pop culture or the media or their friends or even, yes, their teachers.

RISK AND FAILURE VERSUS
RISK AND SUCCESS

"Only those who will risk going too far can
possibly find out how far one can go."
T.S. Eliot

The title of this essay is, in my opinion, the essence of life, as it stands now. Life is pain, and you cannot change that fact. It cannot be regulated by the government. You can take medications so you will not feel the pain, but you are not taking it away; you are only masking it.

Schools outlawing friendships because eventually someone may get hurt. The NFL changing the game so the players will not get hurt. A New York mayor outlaws the size of a soda you can purchase so you will not get hurt. Where does it end? What happens if this continues? What happens to our culture if all risk is regulated away? We currently live in a free society, where you can pursue the pleasures and experiences you desire. Some people like to mountain climb, a somewhat dangerous pastime. Some people like to SCUBA dive, another dangerous pastime. How about flying, hang gliding, bungee jumping, skydiving, surfing, skiing, mountain biking, or walking across the street on a Friday night to get to a bar? Should all of these activities be outlawed?

I want to protect my children. If it were up to me, I would prefer they never experience pain or heartache. However, I wouldn't want that at the expense of them experiencing relationships containing love and affection, knowing full well many of those potential relationships will end in heartache, I still wouldn't deny them the opportunity to experience it for themselves. In my opinion, to do so would be to rob them of their humanity.

We could wrap ourselves and our children up in a cocoon, attempting to protect them from everything. But there is danger in doing so. We run the risk of raising people who are afraid to take risks. Life is life because of risks. Can you imagine a world where no one took any risks? How would you expect anyone to succeed at anything? No one would even try.

DON'T LIKES

- I don't like hang-ups on my answering machine.
- I don't like leaving messages on answering machines.
- I don't like it when I write people a letter and they call me to tell me they received it rather than write me back.
- I don't like to wake up in the morning.
- I don't like to wake up other people. (In the military they actually teach you how to wake people up. I am not kidding.)
- I do not like the term "wake up." I think it is too harsh. They should change it to "ease into the day."
- Whoever "they" are, I don't like them.
- I don't like the fact our society has become so soft that we feel the need to change words and phrases to gentler words and phrases, for political correctness.
- People who drag their flip-flops while walking annoy me. Actually, persons who drag their feet annoy me. Actually, people who walk too slowly in front of me annoy me.
- I don't like being annoyed.

OATHS, PRAYERS, AND OTHER THOUGHTS

Below is the International Association of Chiefs of Police Oath of Honor. I first heard it in the Border Patrol Academy in 1997. One of the instructors was a member of this association. It has stuck with me through the years in all the different agencies for which I have worked. It is a powerful oath and something that made me realize the authority with which I was entrusted was not something to be taken lightly.

> On my honor I will never betray my badge, my integrity, my character, or the public trust. I will always have the courage to hold myself and others accountable for our actions and I will always uphold the Constitution and community I serve.

Perhaps I am the youngest cynic in the world to have such low opinions of most of our elected officials. Imagine if our political leaders held themselves to the standards mentioned in the oath above, knowing this sounds very "Mr. Smith Goes to Washington." Just think how much better our country, or even our society as a whole, would be. Let us take it one step further. Imagine if everyone held themselves to this standard. Now, that is really a stretch, not only because there will always be criminals and evil people, but human beings are typically selfish and motivated by the things which flow contrary to an oath such as the one above. Since our elected officials are our representatives, they are a representation of us, the public. Therefore, it should not be surprising to learn of the corruption and self-serving actions of many politicians. Change needs to start somewhere. The easiest thing to change is yourself, which isn't all that easy. But if you want change, it does need a start. I am starting with myself and my children. In that I am attempting to teach my children such things as respect, honor, dignity, and charity. For me, the oath (and the oath I took in the military and as an agent) is an important part of who I am. Admittedly, I am not perfect. In fact, I am very flawed. As my father once said of me, "he is no saint, but he tries." I usually say trying is not enough. Don't just try. Do it. But in this case, trying is the start. Live well, try hard, and do better—not a bad personal philosophy. Perhaps I will try it ... someday.

Since I wrote down the IACP's oath, it seems appropriate to write down some other military/LEO lessons I have picked up along the way in my career.

When I was in the Coast Guard at one of the small boat stations, the following was painted on the wall of the ladder (stairs) leading down to the dock. "You have to go, but you don't have to come back" Morbid, but true. Along the type of saying was the tattoo my Drill Instructor in boot camp had his right forearm. It was a drawing of a skeleton smoking a cigarette and holding a rifle and stated, "Death is Certain, Life is Not."

As a Border Patrol Agent, the following prayer was passed around the Laredo North Station. Reverend Frank J. Hawkins is listed as the author.

A P.A.'s Prayer

Lord, we never asked that You always set things up so that we could cut sign into the sun.

Even when we sweated gallons in the heat and our teeth chattered in the freezing cold, We never asked You to stop the elements just for us.

In the midst of gasoline rationing and budget cuts, we still went through doors, we still jumped the freights, we rode the line. We never expected You to change things just for us.

When one of us or an innocent was wounded or killed, we still trusted in You; even though we didn't always understand.

We just pray, Lord, that You give us grace enough to
live our lives as Your officers as we continue the linewatch
on this side of the Jordan River.

That when we finally get to the High Country,
beyond the timberline,

A place where smugglers don't exist,

Where the water is cool,

The coffee is hot,

And where all of us can shoot one inch groups.

That You'll look at the visa we got at Your embassy
down here and say:

"Welcome home P.A., this is the best detail of your life!"

At the academy when I became a Special Agent, I picked up another prayer.

An L.E. Officer's Prayer

Lord, I ask for courage,

Courage to face and conquer my own fears,

Courage to take me where others will not go.

I ask for strength,

Strength of body to protect others,

And strength of spirit to lead others.

I ask for dedication,

Dedication to my job, to do it well,

Dedication to my community and country, to keep it safe.

And please, Lord. Through it all, be at my side.

In Jesus' name, amen.

Since this essay began with an oath, I will end it with an oath, which
could be considered the most important oath a citizen can take in this
country. It is the oath the president-elect must take before starting the
job. The oath is surprisingly short but surprisingly detailed. It can be
found in Article II, Section 1, eighth paragraph of the US Constitution.

> I do solemnly swear (or affirm) that I will faithfully execute the Office of President of the United States, and will to the best of my ability, preserve, protect and defend the Constitution of the United States.

George Washington said, "So help me God," after he finished the oath in his first inauguration.

Theodore Roosevelt said, "And thus I swear," after he finished the oath.

AFTER DINNER

Religion is very important in my household, "The Sitton House". Unfortunately, it's not the historical "Sitton House" in Pendleton, South Carolina, although my children and I are direct paternal descendants of the original owner. (Side note: The "Sitton House" was the first brick house to be built in the town.) Back to religion. It is helpful to my lovely wife and me as we try to instill morals in our children. Our faith has also helped my lovely wife and me through some of the more challenging aspects of life. Catholicism is important to us, and it is also one of the more forgiving religions, even though it may not seem that way to those who do not practice it. My lovely wife and I often discuss religion and how it relates to what is taking place in today's world. That is not what this essay is about, so do not worry. I am not going to get deep (like a well) here. Consider this essay an easy read.

One evening after dinner, my lovely wife and I were having a discussion, as we often do, and the term "devil's advocate" came up. When I told my lovely wife it was a Roman Catholic term, she looked at me with skepticism in her eyes. Not that I had to prove anything to her (why would I lie to her?), but we looked it up anyway. The definition is "an official appointed to argue against a proposed Beatification or Canonization." It's sort of a different definition from the way we use it today. While looking up "devil's advocate," we came across another term neither of us realized was Roman Catholic: "Dom" (a title given to monks of certain order, especially Benedictines). My lovely wife jokingly said she thought it was short for the champagne or a mafia boss.

Many of the words and terms we use in our everyday lives originated from places we would never expect. Look them up in a dictionary or, if you still have a set in your house, an encyclopedia. (Do you remember when everyone had a set of encyclopedias in the house? If you do, you just "dated" yourself.)

USEFUL WEBSITES

You could say I am old school when it comes to how I like to obtain information. Actually, you could say I am old school about many things and I would take that as a compliment. Thank you. When reading a word I do not recognize, I look it up in the dictionary. (I also underline the word.) When curiosity about something overtakes my desire to do nothing, I look it up in the appropriate encyclopedia. The daily news and headlines are delivered to my home in the form of a newspaper. A thesaurus is on my desk. Yes, you could say I obtain information in an old-school manner.

This does not mean I live in a cave off the grid. Like many people, I find myself spending more time than originally planned surfing the Web. (I would rather be surfing, but the coastal conditions and my location do not always cooperate with my desires.) (The conditions could be applied to other activities, like sex with my lovely wife. Though it should be noted that two of my children had the same September due date, so you can easily tell what two of my Christmas gifts were.) Over the years, I have collected and bookmarked what I consider useful websites. If you are interested, I have included a list of websites with a brief description of the content in the Appendix under "Useful or Interesting Websites."

Many of the sites are for reference, but not all of them. Because my Nana, and one day my children will most likely read this book, I will refrain from listing any adult-only sites. Moreover, all the sites listed are free and do not require you to log in or register.

Happy surfing, but keep in mind it is faster and less distracting to look something up in an encyclopedia. The Internet is like a casino. Once you are in, it is difficult to find the way out. The only difference is I like casinos.

A JUMBLE OF THOUGHTS

- Never let anyone know what you are thinking.
  (That statement sort of goes against the spirit of this book, doesn't it? This entire book is just an inside joke between me and whoever is going to be my recommended therapist.)
- Why do people say, "Not to mention"? What is that about? If you are "not to mention," why are you mentioning it?
- Let your yes be yes. Let your no be no.
- Isn't it interesting that those who hate the rich are those who buy lottery tickets?
- Do you know what your problem is? You have too many problems.
- If you want something done right, you have to know someone who can recommend the right people to hire to do it.
- When driving in front of me, please remember, the vertical pedal on the right makes the vehicle go faster.
- People are too anxious to interject what they are thinking when they should be thinking about what other people are interjecting.
- If you get less than four hours of sleep at night, you are taking a "hate nap."
- Our guiding principle should be the preservation of liberty
- Human values are incompatible with the utopian idea of a perfect society. It is a fallacy which cannot be achieved. Politicians cannot legislate human behavior, and humans are selfish.
- Have you ever noticed politicians most always agree but never at the same time?
- While watching the Republican presidential debate which took place in Las Vegas in 2012, I could not help having a recurring thought. Most of the presidential candidates onstage were not

behaving very presidential. From eye rolling to finger wagging, coupled with interrupting and raising their voices, the candidates acted more like frustrated teenagers than potential leaders of the free world.

- What is more important, what you get or how you get it?
- Falling for a book is a unique experience. If you find out about the author's life through biographies, it makes the novels come alive.
- f you do not like the outcome, you cannot change the rules. You must not. You can change the game you are playing, but do not change the rules of the game. (Some of our elected officials should follow this.)
- People play with other people's emotions like they play their favorite song. They play it and play it until they become sick of it, and then they do not even want to hear it anymore.
- Every conversation, letter, and statement doesn't have to be important, but most of it ought to lead us somewhere.
- We can enjoy it for what it is and sometimes for what it isn't, but never for what it should be.
- Your personality is only a hint at the experiences which have changed you.
- I walk up the stairs to my desk like a person walking toward his church. My desk, the family desk, has become my church, my confessional. All at once I am looking forward to writing and procrastinating.
- Do not measure everything in dollar value, for if you do, you will probably want to return it
- In response to a quote I heard that stated, "A promise is comfort to a fool," I say a fool is someone who takes comfort.
- You realize you are getting older/weaker when the guys from work are going to move something and they do not ask you for help. You realize you are getting even older when you are no longer working.
- I didn't know this, but as a parent you are everything: bookbinder, toy mechanic, and seamstress. (The other day I was sewing a pink ribbon onto a hat.).

- If you take my dreams, then you have taken everything.
- You can take everything but my dreams, but go ahead and take the nightmares.
- Do you realize many younger people do not know what "fast-forward" and "rewind" mean? They "skip" ahead or back. Most would certainly not understand the meaning of the phrase "You sound like a broken record."
- Do younger generations know how to make a collect call or even use a pay phone? Do they know how to call the operator to make an "emergency breakthrough"? Did you know it can only be accomplished using a landline? You cannot make an emergency breakthrough on a cell.
- I never learn. Perhaps, as I have been told, I am stubborn. Or maybe it is like the saying about the dog—no, not that one, the other one.
- I have a dictionary on my desk which has been in my possession since 1993. I am not exactly sure why I started doing this, but I underline every word I look up. There are over twenty years' worth of inquires underlined in this book. It used to, (but no longer), surprises me to find I was looking up a word for the second, third, or fourth time. Apparently I never learn.
- Every man should have a tuxedo (that fits him) in his closet.
- When you're dating, you are really acting like someone you are not until the other person likes you for who you are.
- Enjoy your day. (Say that instead of "Have a good day." I think it has a better ring to it.)
- If it is less than you expected, it is still probably more than you deserve.
- If you ever want to see hypocrisy in action, try driving through the parking lot of a Catholic church after Mass.
- Of course there is time. It may not be enough time, but there is some.
- Do I sound like an angry old man? If so, it is the world that has made me that way. Actually, if so, it is my reaction to the world which has made me that way.

- We could just wrap our children up in a cocoon and have a generation of do-nothings who are afraid to take any risks when their time comes to lead.
- There is danger in children being told everybody is a winner, nothing is ever their fault, and everyone is equal. When they grow up and learn the hard way that there is competition in the world for everything (a job, mate, place to live, and even parking space), they are not prepared.
- Our lives are the results of our choices. This is what I want to teach my children, along with how to wipe your mouth with a napkin.

And the final thought:

- Don't kiss a giraffe while standing in a canoe.

QUOTATIONS

If you know me, you know I love quotes. (If you know me, you also know I have the ability to be irascible, but I will apologize later.) I use quotations in letters and cards. They have been used throughout this book. I use them in conversation. In conversation, the right quotations used at the right time have the ability to make you seem brilliant or, at the very least, interesting. Like most other guys, I often quote lines from movies. (This can be much to the annoyance of my lovely wife, especially if one of my friends joins in the fun.) I have been asked by my wife, and other women, how men are able to remember the lines from an entire scene of a movie. My response is always the same: it is a skill with which most men are born. We can remember the exact lines from an entire scene of a movie, but do not ask us to recite what you told us or said an hour ago. We won't remember.

Listed below are some of my favorite quotations and, at times, little tidbits about the person quoted or how I used the quotation. If you write me a letter, add a quotation. I enjoy them.

I will begin with a quotation from a person who appears in my "List of Important Philosophers." Hopefully the quotation will make you think of this book (perhaps for its content, but maybe not).

> "The reading of all good books is like a conversation
> with the finest men of past centuries."
> —René Descartes

Below are quotations I used in many of the Christmas cards I sent out last year. The receiver of the card determined which quote I used.

"The proper behavior all through the holiday season is to be
drunk. This drunkenness culminates on New Year's Eve, when
you get so drunk you kiss the person you're married to."
—P. J. O'Rourke

I thought it was funny but not very deep (like a well). However, I knew
some of my friends needed or expected a quotation like that from me.
Below is the other quote I used.

"Own only what you can carry with you; know language,
know people. Let your memory be your travel bag."
—Alexander Solzhenitsyn

Alexander Solzhenitsyn was the author of the book *The Gulag
Archipelago*, which is actually three volumes that detail his life and
experiences in the Russian gulag (prison) and work camps. If you ever
want to feel better about your life or if you ever want to feel depressed, read
them. Just don't do it with a bottle of vodka; you may end up thinking really
depressing thoughts. It is similar to reading the book of Job in the Bible.

"One of the common failings among honorable people is a
failure to appreciate how thoroughly dishonorable some other
people can be, and how dangerous it is to trust them."
—Thomas Sowell

"Think like a man of action. Act like a man of thought."
—Henri Bergson

"Freedom, after all, is simply being able to live
with the consequences of your decisions."
—James X. Mullen

"How strangely will the tools of a tyrant pervert
the plain meaning of words?"
Samuel Adams

111

The following quote is on a placard in Disney World. It is located in the garden which surrounds the Tea-Cup ride in Fantasyland.

"Be good at something.
It makes you valuable.
Have something to bring to the table
because that will make you more welcome."
—Randy Pausch

"If you wish to make an apple pie truly from
scratch, you must first invent the universe."
—Carl Sagan

"What is the recipe for successful achievement? To my
mind there are just four essential ingredients: Choose
a career you love, give it the best there is in you, seize
your opportunities, and be a member of the team"
—Benjamin F. Fairless

"One glance at a book and you hear the voice of
another person, perhaps someone dead for 1,000
years. To read is to voyage through time."
—Carl Sagan

"When you read a book, you spend hours in intimate contact
with the mind of another person. It's an intense but one-
sided relationship. A reader knowing who we really are is
guaranteed to find us disappointing. The experience of a
book is so much better than the experience of a person."
—Justin Cronin

To end this book, I knew I needed the perfect quotation, something that sums up my jumble of thoughts perfectly without my having to actually come up with an ending myself. Therefore, I will leave it up to Walter Gropius.

> "If your contribution has been vital there will
> always be somebody to pick up where you left off,
> and that will be your claim to immortality."
> —Walter Gropius

The End

A JUMBLE OF THOUGHTS

APPENDEX TABLE OF CONTENTS

- H.R. 747
- H.R. 748
- U.S. Senate and Congress Phone List
- Important or At Least Interesting Dates
- Hazard Lights
- Important Philosophers
- Clichés
- Web Sites

APPENDIX – H.R. 747

I

113TH CONGRESS
1ST SESSION

H. R. 747

To amend the Military Selective Service Act to require the registration of women with the Selective Service System in light of the Department of Defense elimination of the rule excluding women from direct ground combat assignments in the Armed Forces.

IN THE HOUSE OF REPRESENTATIVES

FEBRUARY 15, 2013

Mr. RANGEL (for himself and Mr. MORAN) introduced the following bill; which was referred to the Committee on Armed Services

---

A BILL

To amend the Military Selective Service Act to require the registration of women with the Selective Service System in light of the Department of Defense elimination of the rule excluding women from direct ground combat assignments in the Armed Forces.

1   *Be it enacted by the Senate and House of Representa-*

2   *tives of the United States of America in Congress assembled,*

SECTION 1. NONDISCRIMINATION IN APPLICATION OF MILITARY SELECTIVE SERVICE REGISTRATION REQUIREMENT FOR CITIZENS AND CERTAIN RESIDENTS OF THE UNITED STATES.

(a) APPLICABILITY TO ALL CITIZENS AND RESIDENTS WITHIN SPECIFIED AGE RANGE.—Section 3(a) of the Military Selective Service Act (50 U.S.C. App. 453(a)) is amended—

    (1) in the first sentence—

        (A) by striking "male" both places it appears; and

        (B) by inserting "or herself" after "himself"; and

    (2) in the second sentence, by striking "he continues" and inserting "the alien continues".

(b) EFFECTIVE DATE.—The amendments made by subsection (a) shall take effect 60 days after the date of the enactment of this Act.

○

I

113TH CONGRESS
1ST SESSION

H. R. 748

To require all persons in the United States between the ages of 18 and 25 to perform national service, either as a member of the uniformed services or as civilian service in a Federal, State, or local government program or with a community-based agency or community-based entity, to authorize the induction of persons in the uniformed services during wartime to meet end-strength requirements of the uniformed services, to provide for the registration of women under the Military Selective Service Act, and for other purposes.

IN THE HOUSE OF REPRESENTATIVES

FEBRUARY 15, 2013

Mr. RANGEL introduced the following bill; which was referred to the Committee on Armed Services

---

A BILL

To require all persons in the United States between the ages of 18 and 25 to perform national service, either as a member of the uniformed services or as civilian service in a Federal, State, or local government program or with a community-based agency or community-based entity, to authorize the induction of persons in the uniformed services during wartime to meet end-strength requirements of the uniformed services, to provide for the registration of women under the Military Selective Service Act, and for other purposes.

119

1   *Be it enacted by the Senate and House of Representa-*

2   *tives of the United States of America in Congress assembled,*

3   **SECTION 1. SHORT TITLE; TABLE OF CONTENTS.**

4   (a) SHORT TITLE.—This Act may be cited as the

5   "Universal National Service Act".

6   (b) TABLE OF CONTENTS.—The table of contents for

7   this Act is as follows:

8   # TITLE I—NATIONAL SERVICE

9   **SEC. 101. DEFINITIONS.**

10   In this title:

11   (1) The terms "community-based agency" and

12   "community-based entity" have the meanings given

13   those terms in section 101 of the National and Com-

14   munity Service Act of 1990 (42 U.S.C. 12511).

15   (2) The term "contingency operation" has the

16   meaning given that term in section 101(a)(13) of

17   title 10, United States Code.

1   (3) The term "military service" means service

2 performed as a member of an active or reserve com-

3 ponent of the uniformed services.

4   (4) The term "national service" means—

5   (A) military service; or

6   (B) civilian service in a Federal, State, or

7   local government program or with a commu-

8   nity-based agency or community-based entity

9   that, as determined by the President, is en-

10   gaged in meeting human, educational, environ-

11   mental, or public safety needs.

12   (5) The term "Secretary concerned" means—

13   (A) the Secretary of Defense with respect

14   to the Army, Navy, Air Force, and Marine

15   Corps;

16   (B) the Secretary of Homeland Security

17   with respect to the Coast Guard;

18   (C) the Secretary of Commerce with re-

19   spect to the National Oceanic and Atmospheric

20   Administration; and

21   (D) the Secretary of Health and Human

22   Services with respect to the Public Health Serv-

23   ice.

24   (6) The term "United States", when used in a

25 geographical sense, means the several States, the

1   District of Columbia, Puerto Rico, the Virgin Is-

2   lands, and Guam.

3   (7) The term "uniformed services" means the

4   Army, Navy, Air Force, Marine Corps, Coast Guard,

5   commissioned corps of the National Oceanic and At-

6   mospheric Administration, and commissioned corps

7   of the Public Health Service.

SEC. 102. NATIONAL SERVICE OBLIGATION.

9   (a) OBLIGATION FOR SERVICE.—It is the obligation

10   of every citizen of the United States, and every other per-

11   son residing in the United States, who is between the ages

12   of 18 and 25 to perform a period of national service as

13   prescribed in this title unless exempted under the provi-

14   sions of this title.

15   (b) FORMS OF NATIONAL SERVICE.—The national

16   service obligation under this title shall be performed either

17   through—

18   (1) military service; or

19   (2) civilian service in a Federal, State, or local

20   government program or with a community-based

21   agency or community-based entity that, as deter-

22   mined by the President, is engaged in meeting

23   human, educational, environmental, or public safety

24   needs.

1   (c) AGE LIMITS.—A person may be inducted under
2 this title only if the person has attained the age of 18
3 and has not attained the age of 25.

4 **SEC. 103. INDUCTION TO PERFORM NATIONAL SERVICE.**

5   (a) INDUCTION REQUIREMENTS.—The President
6 shall provide for the induction of persons described in sec-
7 tion 102(a) to perform their national service obligation.

8   (b) LIMITATION ON INDUCTION FOR MILITARY SERV-
9 ICE.—Persons described in section 102(a) may be in-
10 ducted to perform military service only if—

11   (1) a declaration of war is in effect;

12   (2) the President declares a national emer-
13   gency, which the President determines necessitates
14   the induction of persons to perform military service,
15   and immediately informs Congress of the reasons for
16   the declaration and the need to induct persons for
17   military service; or

18   (3) members of the Army, Navy, Air Force, or
19   Marine Corps are engaged in a contingency oper-
20   ation pursuant to a congressional authorization for
21   the use of military force.

22   (c) LIMITATION ON NUMBER OF PERSONS INDUCTED
23 FOR MILITARY SERVICE.—When the induction of persons
24 for military service is authorized by subsection (b), the
25 President shall determine the number of persons described

1 in section 102(a) whose national service obligation is to
2 be satisfied through military service based on—

3   (1) the authorized end strengths of the uni-
4   formed services; and

5   (2) the feasibility of the uniformed services to
6   recruit sufficient volunteers to achieve such end-
7   strength levels.

8 (d) SELECTION FOR INDUCTION.—

9   (1) RANDOM SELECTION FOR MILITARY SERV-
10   ICE.—When the induction of persons for military
11   service is authorized by subsection (b), the President
12   shall utilize a mechanism for the random selection of
13   persons to be inducted to perform military service.

14   (2) RANDOM SELECTION FOR CIVILIAN SERV-
15   ICE.—Persons described in section 102(a) who do
16   not volunteer to perform military service or are not
17   inducted for military service shall perform their na-
18   tional service obligation in a civilian capacity pursu-
19   ant to section 102(b)(2).

20 (e) VOLUNTARY SERVICE.—A person subject to in-
21 duction under this title may—

22   (1) volunteer to perform national service in lieu
23   of being inducted; or

1   (2) request permission to be inducted at a time

2   other than the time at which the person is otherwise

3   called for induction.

4 **SEC. 104. TWO-YEAR PERIOD OF NATIONAL SERVICE.**

5   (a) GENERAL RULE.—Except as otherwise provided

6 in this section, the period of national service performed

7 by a person under this title shall be two years.

8   (b) GROUNDS FOR EXTENSION.—At the discretion of

9 the President, the period of military service for a member

10 of the uniformed services under this title may be ex-

11 tended—

12   (1) with the consent of the member, for the

13   purpose of furnishing hospitalization, medical, or

14   surgical care for injury or illness incurred in line of

15   duty; or

16   (2) for the purpose of requiring the member to

17   compensate for any time lost to training for any

18   cause.

19   (c) EARLY TERMINATION.—The period of national

20 service for a person under this title shall be terminated

21 before the end of such period under the following cir-

22 cumstances:

23   (1) The voluntary enlistment and active service

24   of the person in an active or reserve component of

25   the uniformed services for a period of at least two

1   years, in which case the period of basic military

2   training and education actually served by the person

3   shall be counted toward the term of enlistment.

4   (2) The admission and service of the person as

5   a cadet or midshipman at the United States Military

6   Academy, the United States Naval Academy, the

7   United States Air Force Academy, the Coast Guard

8   Academy, or the United States Merchant Marine

9   Academy.

10   (3) The enrollment and service of the person in

11   an officer candidate program, if the person has

12   signed an agreement to accept a Reserve commission

13   in the appropriate service with an obligation to serve

14   on active duty if such a commission is offered upon

15   completion of the program.

16   (4) Such other grounds as the President may

17   establish.

18 **SEC. 105. IMPLEMENTATION BY THE PRESIDENT.**

19   (a) IN GENERAL.—The President shall prescribe

20 such regulations as are necessary to carry out this title.

21   (b) MATTER TO BE COVERED BY REGULATIONS.—

22 Such regulations shall include specification of the fol-

23 lowing:

(1) The types of civilian service that may be performed in order for a person to satisfy the person's national service obligation under this title.

(2) The types of Federal, State, and local government programs and programs carried out by a community-based agency or community-based entity that may be used for the performance of national service.

(3) Standards for satisfactory performance of civilian service and of penalties for failure to perform civilian service satisfactorily.

(4) The manner in which persons shall be selected for induction under this title, including the manner in which those selected will be notified of such selection.

(5) All other administrative matters in connection with the induction of persons under this title and the registration, examination, and classification of such persons.

(6) A means to determine questions or claims with respect to inclusion for, or exemption or deferment from induction under this title, including questions of conscientious objection.

1   (7) Standards for compensation and benefits

2   for persons performing their national service obliga-

3   tion under this title through civilian service.

4   (8) Such other matters as the President deter-

5   mines necessary to carry out this title.

6   (c) USE OF PRIOR ACT.—To the extent determined

7 appropriate by the President, the President may use for

8 purposes of this title the procedures provided in the Mili-

9 tary Selective Service Act (50 U.S.C. App. 451 et seq.),

10 including procedures for registration, selection, and induc-

11 tion.

12 **SEC. 106. EXAMINATION AND CLASSIFICATION OF PER-**

13   **SONS.**

14   (a) EXAMINATION.—Every person subject to induc-

15 tion under this title shall, before induction, be physically

16 and mentally examined and shall be classified as to fitness

17 to perform national service.

18   (b) DIFFERENT CLASSIFICATION STANDARDS.—The

19 President may apply different classification standards for

20 fitness for military service and fitness for civilian service.

21 **SEC. 107. DEFERMENTS AND POSTPONEMENTS.**

22   (a) HIGH SCHOOL STUDENTS.—A person who is pur-

23 suing a standard course of study, on a full-time basis, in

24 a secondary school or similar institution of learning shall

1 be entitled to have induction under this title postponed
2 until the person—

3   (1) obtains a high school diploma;

4   (2) ceases to pursue satisfactorily such course
5   of study; or

6   (3) attains the age of 20.

7   (b) POST SECONDARY STUDENTS.—A person who is
8 pursuing a standard course of study, on a full-time basis,
9 in a university, technical school or similar institution of
10 learning shall be entitled to have induction under this title
11 postponed until the person—

12   (1) obtains a certificate or diploma;

13   (2) ceases to pursue satisfactorily such course
14   of study; or

15   (3) attains the age of 24.

16   (c) HARDSHIP AND DISABILITY.—Deferments from
17 national service under this title may be made for—

18   (1) extreme hardship; or

19   (2) physical or mental disability.

20   (d) TRAINING CAPACITY.—The President may post-
21 pone or suspend the induction of persons for military serv-
22 ice under this title as necessary to limit the number of
23 persons receiving basic military training and education to
24 the maximum number that can be adequately trained.

•HR 748 IH

1   (e) TERMINATION.—No deferment or postponement
2 of induction under this title shall continue after the cause
3 of such deferment or postponement ceases.

4 **SEC. 108. INDUCTION EXEMPTIONS.**

5   (a) QUALIFICATIONS.—No person may be inducted
6 for military service under this title unless the person is
7 acceptable to the Secretary concerned for training and
8 meets the same health and physical qualifications applica-
9 ble under section 505 of title 10, United States Code, to
10 persons seeking original enlistment in a regular compo-
11 nent of the Armed Forces.

12   (b) OTHER MILITARY SERVICE.—No person shall be
13 liable for induction under this title who—

14   (1) is serving, or has served honorably for at
15   least six months, in any component of the uniformed
16   services on active duty; or

17   (2) is or becomes a cadet or midshipman at the
18   United States Military Academy, the United States
19   Naval Academy, the United States Air Force Acad-
20   emy, the Coast Guard Academy, the United States
21   Merchant Marine Academy, a midshipman of a Navy
22   accredited State maritime academy, a member of the
23   Senior Reserve Officers' Training Corps, or the
24   naval aviation college program, so long as that per-

1   son satisfactorily continues in and completes at least

2   two years training therein.

3   **SEC. 109. CONSCIENTIOUS OBJECTION.**

4   (a) CLAIMS AS CONSCIENTIOUS OBJECTOR.—Noth-

5   ing in this title shall be construed to require a person to

6   be subject to combatant training and service in the uni-

7   formed services, if that person, by reason of sincerely held

8   moral, ethical, or religious beliefs, is conscientiously op-

9   posed to participation in war in any form.

10   (b) ALTERNATIVE NONCOMBATANT OR CIVILIAN

11   SERVICE.—A person who claims exemption from combat-

12   ant training and service under subsection (a) and whose

13   claim is sustained by the local board shall—

14   (1) be assigned to noncombatant service (as de-

15   fined by the President), if the person is inducted

16   into the uniformed services; or

17   (2) be ordered by the local board, if found to

18   be conscientiously opposed to participation in such

19   noncombatant service, to perform civilian service for

20   the period specified in section 104(a) and subject to

21   such regulations as the President may prescribe.

22   **SEC. 110. DISCHARGE FOLLOWING NATIONAL SERVICE.**

23   (a) DISCHARGE.—Upon completion or termination of

24   the obligation to perform national service under this title,

25   a person shall be discharged from the uniformed services

1 or from civilian service, as the case may be, and shall not

2 be subject to any further service under this title.

3 　　　(b) COORDINATION WITH OTHER AUTHORITIES.—

4 Nothing in this section shall limit or prohibit the call to

5 active service in the uniformed services of any person who

6 is a member of a regular or reserve component of the uni-

7 formed services.

8 TITLE II—AMENDMENTS TO
9 MILITARY SELECTIVE SERV-
10 ICE ACT

11 **SEC. 201. REGISTRATION OF FEMALES.**

12 　　　(a) REGISTRATION REQUIRED.—Section 3(a) of the

13 Military Selective Service Act (50 U.S.C. 453(a)) is

14 amended—

15 　　　　　(1) by striking "male" both places it appears;

16 　　　　　(2) by inserting "or herself" after "himself";

17 　　and

18 　　　　　(3) by striking "he" and inserting "the per-

19 　　son".

20 　　　(b) CONFORMING AMENDMENT.—Section 16(a) of

21 the Military Selective Service Act (50 U.S.C. App. 466(a))

22 is amended by striking "men" and inserting "persons".

1 **SEC. 202. REGISTRATION AND INDUCTION AUTHORITY.**

2   (a) REGISTRATION.—Section 4 of the Military Selec-
3 tive Service Act (50 U.S.C. App. 454) is amended by in-
4 serting after subsection (g) the following new subsection:

5   "(h) This section does not apply with respect to the
6 induction of persons into the Armed Forces pursuant to
7 the Universal National Service Act.".

8   (b) INDUCTION.—Section 17(c) of the Military Selec-
9 tive Service Act (50 U.S.C. App. 467(c)) is amended by
10 striking "now or hereafter" and all that follows through
11 the period at the end and inserting "inducted pursuant
12 to the Universal National Service Act.".

○

UNITED STATES SENATE
113th Congress Telephone List

Any updates to the list can be found at the following web site: http://www.senate.gov/general/contact_information/senators_cfm.cfm

Vice President BIDEN, Jr., Joseph R. (202) 224-2424

ALEXANDER, Lamar (R-TN) (202) 224-4944

AYOTTE, Kelly (R-NH) (202) 224-3324

BALDWIN, Tammy (D-WI) (202) 224-5653

BARRASSO, John (R-WY) (202) 224-6441

BAUCUS, Max (D-MT) (202) 224-2651

BEGICH, Mark (D-AK) (202) -3004

BENNET, Michael F. (D-CO) (202) 224-5852

BLUMENTHAL, Richard (D-CT) (202) 224-2823

BLUNT, Roy (R-MO) (202) 224-5721

BOOZMAN, John (R-AR) (202) 224-4843

BOXER, Barbara (D-CA) (202) 224-3553

BROWN, Sherrod (D-OH) (202) 224-2315

BURR, Richard (R-NC) (202) 224-3154

CANTWELL, Maria (D-WA) (202) 224-3441

CARDIN, Benjamin L. (D-MD) (202) 224-4524

CARPER, Thomas R. (D-DE) (202) 224-2441

CASEY, Jr., Robert P. (D-PA) (202) 224-6324

CHAMBLISS, Saxby (R-GA) (202) 224-3521

CHIESA, Jeff (R-NJ) (202) 224-3224

COATS, Daniel (R-IN) (202) 224-5623

COBURN, Tom (R-OK) (202) 224-5754

COCHRAN, Thad (R-MS) (202) 224-5054

COLLINS, Susan M. (R-ME) (202) 224-2523

COONS, Christopher A. (D-DE) (202) 224-5042

CORKER, Bob (R-TN) (202) 224-3344

CORNYN, John (R-TX) (202) 224-2934

CRAPO, Mike (R-ID) (202) 224-6142

CRUZ, Ted (R-TX) (202) 224-5922

DONNELLY, Joe (D-IN) 224-4814

DURBIN, Richard J. (D-IL) (202) 224-2152

ENZI, Michael B. (R-WY) (202) 224-3424

FEINSTEIN, Dianne (D-CA) (202) 224-3841

FISCHER, Deb (R-NE) (202) 224-6551

FLAKE, Jeff (R-AZ) (202) 224-4521

FRANKEN, Al (D-MN) (202) 224-5641

GILLIBRAND, Kristen E. (D-NY) (202) 224-4451

GRAHAM, Lindsey (R-SC) (202) 224-5972

GRASSLEY, Chuck (R-IA) (202) 224-3744

HAGAN, Kay R. (D-NC) (202) 224-6342

HARKIN, Tom (D-IA) (202) 224-3254

HATCH, Orrin G. (R-UT) (202) 224-5251

HEINRICH, Martin (D-NM) (202) 224-5521

HEITKAMP, Heidi (D-ND) (202) 224-2043

HELLER, Dean (R-NV) (202) 224-6244

HIRONO, Mazie K. (D-HI) (202) 224-6361

HOEVEN, John (R-ND) (202) 224-2551

INHOFE, James M. (R-OK) (202) 224-4721

ISAKSON, Johnny (R-GA) (202) 224-3643

JOHANNS, Mike (R-NE) (202) 224-4224

JOHNSON, Ron (R-WI) (202) 224-5323

JOHNSON, Tim (D-SD) (202) 224-5842

KAINE, Tim (D-VA) (202) 224-4024

KING, Jr., Angus S. (I-ME) (202) 224-5344

KIRK, Mark (R-IL) (202) 224-2854

KLOBUCHAR, Amy (D-MN) (202) 224-3244

LANDRIEU, Mary L. (D-LA) (202) 224-5824

LEAHY, Patrick J. (D-VT) (202) 224-4242

LEE, Mike (R-UT) (202) 224-5444

LEVIN, Carl (D-MI) (202) 224-6221

MANCHIN III, Joe (D-WV) (202) 224-3954

MARKEY, Edward J. (D-MA) (202) 224-2742

McCAIN, John (R-AZ) (202) 224-2235

McCASKILL, Claire (D-MO) (202) 224-6154

McCONNELL, Mitch (R-KY) (202) 224-2541

MENENDEZ, Robert (D-NJ) (202) 224-4744

MERKLEY, Jeff (D-OR) (202) 224-3753

MIKULSKI, Barbara A. (D-MD) (202) 224-4654

MORAN, Jerry (R-KS) (202) 224-6521

MURKOWSKI, Lisa (R-AK) (202) 224-6665

MURPHY, Christopher (D-CT) (202) 224-4041

MURRAY, Patty (D-WA) (202) 224-2621

NELSON, Bill (D-FL) (202) 224-5274

PAUL, Rand (R-KY) (202) 224-4343

PORTMAN, Rob (R-OH) 224-3353

PRYOR, Mark L. (D-AR) (202) 224-2353

REED, Jack (D-RI) (202) 224-4642

REID, Harry (D-NV) (202) 224-3542

RISCH, James E. (R-ID) (202) 224-2752

ROBERTS, Pat (R-KS) (202) 224-4774

ROCKFELLER IV, John D. (D-WV) (202) 224-6472

RUBIO, Marco (R-FL) (202) 224-3041

SANDERS, Bernard (I-VT) (202) 224-5141

SCHATZ, Brian (D-HI) (202) 224-3934

SHUMMER, Charles E. (D-NY) (202) 224-6542

SCOTT, Tim (R-SC) (202) 224-6121

SESSIONS, Jeff (R-AL) (202) 224-4124

SHAHEEN, Jeanne (D-NH) (202) 224-2841

SHELBY, Richard C. (R-AL) (202) 224-5744

STABENOW, Debbie (D-MI) (202) 224-4822

TESTER, Jon (D-MT) (202) 224-2644

THUNE, John (R-SD) (202) 224-2321

TOOMEY, Patrick J. (R-PA) (202) 224-4254

UDALL, Mark (D-CO) (202) 224-5941

UDALL, Tom (D-NM) (202) 224-6621

VITTER, David (R-LA) (202) 224-4623

WARNER, Mark R. (D-VA) (202) 224-2023
WARREN, Elizabeth (D-MA) (202) 224-4543
WHITEHOUSE, Sheldon (D-RI) (202) 224-2921
WICKER, Roger F. (R-MS) (202) 224-6253
WYDEN, Ron (D-OR) (202) 224-5244

Any updates to the list can be found at the following web site: http://www.senate.gov/general/contact_information/senators_cfm.cfm

113th CONGRESS
UNITED STATES HOUSE OF REPRESENTAIVES
Telephone list by State

Alabama

Aderholt, Robert (R) (202) 225-4876
Bachus, Spencer (R) (202) 225-4921
Bonner, Jo (R) (202) 225-4931
Brooks, Mo (R) (202) 225-4801
Roby, Martha (R) (202) 225-2901
Rogers (AL), Mike (R) (202) 225-3261
Sewell, Terri A. (D) (202) 225-2665

Alaska

Young, Don (R) (202) 225-5765

American Samoa

Faleomavaega, Eni F. H. (D) (202) 225-8577

Arizona

Barber, Ron (D) (202) 225-2542
Franks, Trent (202) 225-4576
Gosar, Paul A. (R) (202) 225-2315
Grijalva, Raul (D) (202) 225-2435
Kirkpatrick, Ann (D) (202) 225-3361
Pastor, Ed (D) (202) 225-4065

Salmon, Matt (R) (202) 225-2635
Schweikert, David (R) (202) 225-2190
Sinema, Kyrsten (202) 225-9888

Arkansas

Cotton, Tom (R) (202) 225-3772
Crawford, Rick (R) (202) 225-4076
Griffin, Tim (R) (202) 225-2506
Womack, Steve (R) (202) 225-4301

California

Bass, Karen (D) (202) 225-7084
Becerra, Xavier (D) (202) 225-6235
Bera, Ami (D) (202) 225-5716
Brownley, Julia (D) (202) 225-5811
Calvert, Ken (R) (202) 225-1986
Campbell, John (R) (202) 225-5611
Capps, Lois (D) (202) 225-3601
Cárdenas, Tony (D) (202) 225-6131
Chu, Judy (D) (202) 225-5464
Cook, Paul (R) (202) 225-5861
Costa, Jim (D) (202) 225-3341
Davis, Susan (D) (202) 225-2040
Denham, Jeff (R) (202) 225-4540
Eshoo, Anna G. (D) (202) 225-8104
Farr, Sam (D) (202) 225-2861
Garamendi, John (D) (202) 225-1880
Hahn, Janice (D) (202) 225-8220
Honda, Mike (D) (202) 225-2631
Huffman, Jared (D) (202) 225-5161

Hunter, Duncan D. (R) (202) 225-5672

Issa, Darrell (R) (202) 225-3906

LaMalfa, Doug (R) (202) 225-3076

Lee, Barbara (D) (202) 225-2661

Lofgren, Zoe (D) (202) 225-3072

Lowenthal, Alan (D) (202) 225-7924

Matsui, Doris O. (D) (202) 225-7163

McCarthy, Kevin (R) (202) 225-2915

McClintock, Tom (R) (202) 225-2511

McKeon, Buck (R) (202) 225-1956

McNerney, Jerry (D) (202) 225-1947

Miller, Gary (R) (202) 225-3201

Miller, George (D) (202) 225-2095

Napolitano, Grace (D) (202) 225-5256

Negrete McLeod, Gloria (D) (202) 225-6161

Nunes, Devin (R) (202) 225-2523

Pelosi, Nancy (D) (202) 225-4965

Peters, Scott (D) (202) 225-0508

Rohrabacher, Dana (R) (202) 225-2415

Roybal-Allard, Lucille (D) (202) 225-1766

Royce, Ed (R) (202) 225-4111

Ruiz, Raul (D) (202) 225-5330

Sanchez, Linda (D) (202) 225-6676

Sanchez, Loretta (D) (202) 225-2965

Schiff, Adam (D) (202) 225-4176

Sherman, Brad (D) (202) 225-5911

Speier, Jackie (D) (202) 225-3531

Swalwell, Eric (D) (202) 225-5065

Takano, Mark (D) (202) 225-2305

Thompson, Mike (D) (202) 225-3311

Valadao, David (R) (202) 225-4695

Vargas, Juan (D) (202) 225-8045

Waters, Maxine (D) (202) 225-2201

Waxman, Henry (D) (202) 225-3976

Colorado

Coffman, Mike (R) (202) 225-7882
DeGette, Diana (D) (202) 225-4431
Gardner, Cory (R) (202) 225-4676
Lamborn, Doug (R) (202) 225-4422
Perlmutter, Ed (D) (202) 225-2645
Polis, Jared (D) (202) 225-2161
Tipton, Scott (R) (202) 225-4761

Connecticut

Courtney, Joe (D) (202) 225-2076
DeLauro, Rosa L. (D) (202) 225-3661
Esty, Elizabeth (D) (202) 225-4476
Himes, Jim (D) (202) 225-5541
Larson, John B. (D) (202) 225-2265

Delaware

Carney, John (D) (202) 225-4165

District of Columbia

Norton, Eleanor Holmes (D) (202) 225-8050

Florida

Bilirakis, Gus M. (R) (202) 225-5755
Brown, Corrine (D) (202) 225-0123

Buchanan, Vern (R) (202) 225-5015

Castor, Kathy (D) (202) 225-3376

Crenshaw, Ander (R) (202) 225-2501

DeSantis, Ron (R) (202) 225-2706

Deutch, Ted (D) (202) 225-3001

Diaz-Balart, Mario (R) (202) 225-4211

Frankel, Lois (D) (202) 225-9890

Garcia, Joe (D) (202) 225-2778

Grayson, Alan (D) (202) 225-9889

Hastings, Alcee L. (D) (202) 225-1313

Mica, John (R) (202) 225-4035

Miller, Jeff (R) (202) 225-4136

Murphy, Patrick (D) (202) 225-3026

Nugent, Richard (R) (202) 225-1002

Posey, Bill (R) (202) 225-3671

Radel, Trey (R) (202) 225-2536

Rooney, Tom (R) (202) 225-5792

Ros-Lehtinen, Ileana (R) (202) 225-3931

Ross, Dennis (R) (202) 225-1252

Southerland, Steve (R) (202) 225-5235

Wasserman Schultz, Debbie (D) (202) 225-7931

Webster, Daniel (R) (202) 225-2176

Wilson, Frederica (D) (202) 225-4506

Yoho, Ted (R) (202) 225-5744

Young, C.W. Bill (R) (202) 225-5961

Georgia

Barrow, John (D) (202) 225-2823

Bishop Jr., Sanford D. (D) (202) 225-3631

Broun, Paul C. (R) (202) 225-4101

Collins, Doug (R) (202) 225-9893

Gingrey, Phil (R) (202) 225-2931

Graves, Tom (R) (202) 225-5211
Johnson, Henry C. "Hank" Jr. (D) (202) 225-1605
Kingston, Jack (R) (202) 225-5831
Lewis, John (D) (202) 225-3801
Price, Tom (R) (202) 225-4501
Scott, Austin (R) (202) 225-6531
Scott, David (D) (202) 225-2939
Westmoreland, Lynn A. (R) (202) 225-5901
Woodall, Robert (R) (202) 225-4272

Guam

Bordallo, Madeleine (D) (202) 225-1188

Hawaii

Gabbard, Tulsi (D) (202) 225-4906
Hanabusa, Colleen (D) (202) 225-2726

Idaho

Labrador, Raul R. (R) (202) 225-6611
Simpson, Mike (R) (202) 225-5531

Illinois

Bustos, Cheri (D) (202) 225-5905
Davis, Danny K. (D) (202) 225-5006
Davis, Rodney (R) (202) 225-2371
Duckworth, Tammy (D) (202) 225-3711
Enyart, William (D) (202) 225-5661
Foster, Bill (D) (202) 225-3515

Gutierrez, Luis (D) (202) 225-8203
Hultgren, Randy (R) (202) 225-2976
Kelly, Robin (D) (202) 225-0773
Kinzinger, Adam (R) (202) 225-3635
Lipinski, Daniel (D) (202) 225-5701
Quigley, Mike (D) (202) 225-4061
Roskam, Peter J. (R) (202) 225-4561
Rush, Bobby L. (D) (202) 225-4372
Schakowsky, Jan (D) (202) 225-2111
Schneider, Brad (D) (202) 225-4835
Schock, Aaron (R) (202) 225-6201
Shimkus, John (R) (202) 225-5271

Indiana

Brooks, Susan W. (R)   (202) 225-2276
Bucshon, Larry (R) (202) 225-4636
Carson, André (D) (202) 225-4011
Messer, Luke (R) (202) 225-3021
Rokita, Todd (R) (202) 225-5037
Stutzman, Marlin (R) (202) 225-4436
Visclosky, Peter (D) (202) 225-2461
Walorski, Jackie (R) (202) 225-3915
Young, Todd (R) (202) 225-5315

Iowa

Braley, Bruce L. (D) (202) 225-2911
King, Steve (R) (202) 225-4426
Latham, Tom (R) (202) 225-5476
Loebsack, David (D) (202) 225-6576

Kansas

Huelskamp, Tim (R) (202) 225-2715
Jenkins, Lynn (R) (202) 225-6601
Pompeo, Mike (R) (202) 225-6216
Yoder, Kevin (R) (202) 225-2865

Kentucky

Barr, Andy (R) (202) 225-4706
Guthrie, S. Brett (R) (202) 225-3501
Massie, Thomas (R) (202) 225-3465
Rogers, Harold (R) (202) 225-4601
Whitfield, Ed (R) (202) 225-3115
Yarmuth, John A. (D) (202) 225-5401

Louisiana

Alexander, Rodney (R) (202) 225-8490
Boustany Jr., Charles W. (R) (202) 225-2031
Cassidy, William (R) (202) 225-3901
Fleming, John (R) (202) 225-2777
Richmond, Cedric (D) (202) 225-6636
Scalise, Steve (R) (202) 225-3015

Maine

Michaud, Michael (D) (202) 225-6306
Pingree, Chellie (D) (202) 225-6116

Maryland

Cummings, Elijah (D) (202) 225-4741

Delaney, John (D) (202) 225-2721

Edwards, Donna F. (D) (202) 225-8699

Harris, Andy (R) (202) 225-5311

Hoyer, Steny H. (D) (202) 225-4131

Ruppersberger, Dutch (D) (202) 225-3061

Sarbanes, John P. (D) (202) 225-4016

Van Hollen, Chris (D) (202) 225-5341

Massachusetts

Capuano, Michael E. (D) (202) 225-5111

Keating, William (D) (202) 225-3111

Kennedy III, Joseph P. (D) (202) 225-5931

Lynch, Stephen F. (D) (202) 225-8273

Markey, Ed – Vacancy At Time of Printing   (D) (202) 225-2836

McGovern, James (D) (202) 225-6101

Neal, Richard E. (D) (202) 225-5601

Tierney, John (D) (202) 225-8020

Tsongas, Niki (D) (202) 225-3411

Michigan

Amash, Justin (R) (202) 225-3831

Benishek, Dan (R) (202) 225-4735

Bentivolio, Kerry (R) (202) 225-8171

Camp, Dave (R) (202) 225-3561

Conyers Jr., John (D) (202) 225-5126

Dingell, John (D) (202) 225-4071

Huizenga, Bill (R) (202) 225-4401

Kildee, Daniel (D) (202) 225-3611
Levin, Sander (D) (202) 225-4961
Miller, Candice (R) (202) 225-2106
Peters, Gary (D) (202) 225-5802
Rogers, Mike (R) (202) 225-4872
Upton, Fred (R) (202) 225-3761
Walberg, Tim (R) (202) 225-6276

Minnesota

Bachmann, Michele (R) (202) 225-2331
Ellison, Keith (D) (202) 225-4755
Kline, John (R) (202) 225-2271
McCollum, Betty (D) (202) 225-6631
Nolan, Rick (D) (202) 225-6211
Paulsen, Erik (R) (202) 225-2871
Peterson, Collin C. (D) (202) 225-2165
Walz, Timothy J. (D) (202) 225-2472

Mississippi

Harper, Gregg (R) (202) 225-5031
Nunnelee, Alan (R) (202) 225-4306
Palazzo, Steven (R) (202) 225-5772
Thompson, Bennie G. (D) (202) 225-5876

Missouri

Clay Jr., William "Lacy" (D) (202) 225-2406
Cleaver, Emanuel (D) (202) 225-4535
Graves, Sam (R) (202) 225-7041
Hartzler, Vicky (R) (202) 225-2876
Long, Billy (R) (202) 225-6536

Luetkemeyer, Blaine (R) (202) 225-2956
Smith, Jason (R) (202) 225-4404
Wagner, Ann (R) (202) 225-1621

Montana

Daines, Steve (R) (202) 225-3211

Nebraska

Fortenberry, Jeff (R) (202) 225-4806
Terry, Lee (R) (202) 225-4155
Smith, Adrian (R) (202) 225-6435

Nevada

Amodei, Mark (R) (202) 225-6155
Heck, Joe (R) (202) 225-3252
Horsford, Steven (D) (202) 225-9894
Titus, Dina (D) (202) 225-5965

New Hampshire

Kuster, Ann (D) (202) 225-5206
Shea-Porter, Carol (D) (202) 225-5456

New Jersey

Andrews, Robert E. (D) (202) 225-6501
Frelinghuysen, Rodney (R) (202) 225-5034
Garrett, Scott (R) (202) 225-4465
Holt, Rush (D) (202) 225-5801

Lance, Leonard (R) (202) 225-5361

LoBiondo, Frank (R) (202) 225-6572

Pallone Jr., Frank (D) (202) 225-4671

Pascrell Jr., Bill (D) (202) 225-5751

Payne Jr., Donald (D) (202) 225-3436

Runyan, Jon (R) (202) 225-4765

Sires, Albio (D) (202) 225-7919

Smith, Chris (R) (202) 225-3765

New Mexico

Lujan Grisham, Michelle (D) (202) 225-6316

Lujan, Ben R. (D) (202) 225-6190

Pearce, Steve (R) (202) 225-2365

New York

Bishop, Timothy (D) (202) 225-3826

Clarke, Yvette D. (D) (202) 225-6231

Collins, Chris (R) (202) 225-5265

Crowley, Joseph (D) (202) 225-3965

Engel, Eliot (D) (202) 225-2464

Gibson, Chris (R) (202) 225-5614

Grimm, Michael (R) (202) 225-3371

Hanna, Richard (R) (202) 225-3665

Higgins, Brian (D) (202) 225-3306

Israel, Steve (D) (202) 225-3335

Jeffries, Hakeem (D) (202) 225-5936

King, Pete (R) (202) 225-7896

Lowey, Nita (D) (202) 225-6506

Maffei, Daniel (D) (202) 225-3701

Maloney, Carolyn (D) (202) 225-7944

Maloney, Sean Patrick (D) (202) 225-5441
McCarthy, Carolyn (D) (202) 225-5516
Meeks, Gregory W. (D) (202) 225-3461
Meng, Grace (D) (202) 225-2601
Nadler, Jerrold (D) (202) 225-5635
Owens, Bill (D) (202) 225-4611
Rangel, Charles B. (D) (202) 225-4365
Reed, Tom (R) (202) 225-3161
Serrano, José E. (D) (202) 225-4361
Slaughter, Louise (D) (202) 225-3615
Tonko, Paul D. (D) (202) 225-5076
Velázquez, Nydia M. (D) (202) 225-2361

North Carolina

Butterfield, G.K. (D) (202) 225-3101
Coble, Howard (R) (202) 225-3065
Ellmers, Renee (R) (202) 225-4531
Foxx, Virginia (R) (202) 225-2071
Holding, George (R) (202) 225-3032
Hudson, Richard (R) (202) 225-3715
Jones, Walter B. (R) (202) 225-3415
McHenry, Patrick T. (R) (202) 225-2576
McIntyre, Mike (D) (202) 225-2731
Meadows, Mark (R) (202) 225-6401
Pittenger, Robert (R) (202) 225-1976
Price, David (D) (202) 225-1784
Watt, Mel (D) (202) 225-1510

North Dakota

Cramer, Kevin (R) (202) 225-2611

Northern Mariana Islands

Sablan, Gregorio (D) (202) 225-2646

Ohio

Beatty, Joyce (D) (202) 225-4324
Boehner, John A. (R) (202) 225-6205
Chabot, Steve (R) (202) 225-2216
Fudge, Marcia L. (D) (202) 225-7032
Gibbs, Bob (R) (202) 225-6265
Johnson, Bill (R) (202) 225-5705
Jordan, Jim (R) (202) 225-2676
Joyce, David (R) (202) 225-5731
Kaptur, Marcy (D) (202) 225-4146
Latta, Robert E. (R) (202) 225-6405
Renacci, Jim (R) (202) 225-3876
Ryan, Tim (D) (202) 225-5261
Stivers, Steve (R) (202) 225-2015
Tiberi, Pat (R) (202) 225-5355
Turner, Michael (R) (202) 225-6465
Wenstrup, Brad (R) (202) 225-3164

Oklahoma

Bridenstine, Jim (R) (202) 225-2211
Cole, Tom (R) (202) 225-6165
Lankford, James (R) (202) 225-2132
Lucas, Frank (R) (202) 225-5565
Mullin, Markwayne (R) (202) 225-2701

Oregon

Blumenauer, Earl (D) (202) 225-4811
Bonamici, Suzanne (D) (202) 225-0855
DeFazio, Peter (D) (202) 225-6416
Schrader, Kurt (D) (202) 225-5711
Walden, Greg (R) (202) 225-6730

Pennsylvania

Barletta, Lou (R) (202) 225-6511
Brady, Robert (D) (202) 225-4731
Cartwright, Matthew (D) (202) 225-5546
Dent, Charles W. (R) (202) 225-6411
Doyle, Mike (D) (202) 225-2135
Fattah, Chaka (D) (202) 225-4001
Fitzpatrick, Michael G. (R) (202) 225-4276
Gerlach, Jim (R) (202) 225-4315
Kelly, Mike (R) (202) 225-5406
Marino, Tom (R) (202) 225-3731
Meehan, Pat (R) (202) 225-2011
Murphy, Tim (R) (202) 225-2301
Perry, Scott (R) (202) 225-5836
Pitts, Joseph R. (R) (202) 225-2411
Rothfus, Keith (R) (202) 225-2065
Schwartz, Allyson Y. (D) (202) 225-6111
Shuster, Bill (R) (202)-225-2431
Thompson, Glenn W. (R) (202) 225-5121

Puerto Rico

Pierluisi, Pedro (D) (202) 225-2615

Rhode Island

Cicilline, David (D) (202) 225-4911
Langevin, Jim (D) (202) 225-2735

South Carolina

Clyburn, James E. (D) (202) 225-3315
Duncan, Jeff (R) (202) 225-5301
Gowdy, Trey (R) (202) 225-6030
Mulvaney, Mick (R) (202) 225-5501
Rice, Tom (R) (202) 225-9895
Sanford, Mark (R) (202) 225-3176
Wilson, Joe (R) (202) 225-2452

South Dakota

Noem, Kristi (R) (202) 225-2801

Tennessee

Black, Diane (R) (202) 225-4231
Blackburn, Marsha (R) (202) 225-2811
Cohen, Steve (D) (202) 225-3265
Cooper, Jim (D) (202) 225-4311
DesJarlais, Scott (R) (202) 225-6831
Duncan Jr., John J. (R) (202) 225-5435
Fincher, Stephen (R) (202) 225-4714
Fleischmann, Chuck (R) (202) 225-3271
Roe, Phil (R) (202) 225-6356

Texas

Barton, Joe (R) (202) 225-2002

Brady, Kevin (R) (202) 225-4901

Burgess, Michael (R) (202) 225-7772

Carter, John (R) (202) 225-3864

Castro, Joaquin (D) (202) 225-3236

Conaway, K. Michael (R) (202) 225-3605

Cuellar, Henry (D) (202) 225-1640

Culberson, John (R) (202) 225-2571

Doggett, Lloyd (D) (202) 225-4865

Farenthold, Blake (R) (202) 225-7742

Flores, Bill (R) (202) 225-6105

Gallego, Pete (D) (202) 225-4511

Gohmert, Louie (R) (202) 225-3035

Granger, Kay (R) (202) 225-5071

Green, Al (D) (202) 225-7508

Green, Gene (D) (202) 225-1688

Hall, Ralph M. (R) (202) 225-6673

Hensarling, Jeb (R) (202) 225-3484

Hinojosa, Rubén (D) (202) 225-2531

Jackson Lee, Sheila (D) (202) 225-3816

Johnson, Eddie Bernice (D) (202) 225-8885

Johnson, Sam (R) (202) 225-4201

Marchant, Kenny (R) (202) 225-6605

McCaul, Michael T. (R) (202) 225-2401

Neugebauer, Randy (R) (202) 225-4005

Olson, Pete (R) (202) 225-5951

O'Rourke, Beto (D) (202) 225-4831

Poe, Ted (R) (202) 225-6565

Sessions, Pete (R) (202) 225-2231

Smith, Lamar (R) (202) 225-4236

Stockman, Steve (R) (202) 225-1555

Thornberry, Mac (R) (202) 225-3706

Veasey, Marc (D) (202) 225-9897

Vela, Filemon (D) (202) 225-9901
Weber, Randy (R) (202) 225-2831
Williams, Roger (R) (202) 225-9896

Utah

Bishop, Rob (R) (202) 225-0453
Chaffetz, Jason (R) (202) 225-7751
Matheson, Jim (D) (202) 225-3011
Stewart, Chris (R) (202) 225-9730

Vermont

Welch, Peter (D) (202) 225-4115

Virgin Islands

Christensen, Donna M., (D) (202) 225-1790

Virginia

Wittman, Robert J. (R) (202) 225-4261
Rigell, Scott (R) (202) 225-4215
Scott, Robert C. (D) (202) 225-8351
Forbes, J. Randy (R) (202) 225-6365
Hurt, Robert (R) (202) 225-4711
Goodlatte, Bob (R) (202) 225-5431
Cantor, Eric (R) (202) 225-2815
Moran, James (D) (202) 225-4376
Griffith, Morgan (R) (202) 225-3861
Wolf, Frank (R) (202) 225-5136
Connolly, Gerald E. "Gerry" (D) (202) 225-1492

Washington

DelBene, Suzan (D) (202) 225-6311

Larsen, Rick (D) (202) 225-2605

Herrera Beutler, Jaime (R) (202) 225-3536

Hastings, Doc (R) (202) 225-5816

McMorris Rodgers, Cathy (R) (202) 225-2006

Kilmer, Derek (D) (202) 225-5916

McDermott, Jim (D) (202) 225-3106

Reichert, David G. (R) (202) 225-7761

Smith, Adam (D) (202) 225-8901

Heck, Denny (D) (202) 225-9740

West Virginia

McKinley, David (R) (202) 225-4172

Capito, Shelley Moore (R) (202) 225-2711

Rahall, Nick (D) (202) 225-3452

Wisconsin

Ryan, Paul (R) (202) 225-3031

Pocan, Mark (D) (202) 225-2906

Kind, Ron (D) (202) 225-5506

Moore, Gwen (D) (202) 225-4572

Sensenbrenner, F. James (R) (202) 225-5101

Petri, Thomas (R) (202) 225-2476

Duffy, Sean P. (R) (202) 225-3365

Ribble, Reid (R) (202) 225-5665

Wyoming

Lummis, Cynthia M. (R) (202) 225-2311

APPENDIX –
IMPORTANT OR AT LEAST
INTERESTING DATES

January 1, 1908 – 1st ball dropped at Times Square in New York City

January 2, 1870 – Construction of Brooklyn Bridge begins

January 9, 1861 – Mississippi secedes from the Union

January 10, 1861 – Florida secedes from the Union

January 11, 1861 – Alabama secedes from the Union

January 12, 1966 – Batman debuts on television

January 13, 1957 – Frisbee Invented

January 14, 1973 – Miami Dolphins defeat the Redskins in Superbowl VII and become 1st undeafeated team in NFL history

January 14, 1990 – The Simpsons debuts on television

January 15, 1967 – First Super Bowl

January 19, 1861 – Georgia secedes from the Union

January 20 – Inauguration Day

January 20 – St. Agnes Day – The night when, according to legend, a woman dreams of her future husband

January 21, 1915 – 1st Kiwanis Club Chartered

January 21, 1976 – First flight of the Concord

January 22, 1905 – Bloody Sunday, Russia

January 24, 1935 – Beer was first sold in cans

January 26, 1861 – Louisiana secedes from the Union

February 1, 1861 – Texas secedes from the Union

February 4, 1789 – First U.S. President Elected

February 6, 1952 – Elizabeth II ascends to the UK throne

February 7, 1964 – Beginning of the first U.S. Beatles tour

February 8, 1910 – Boy Scouts founded

February 10, 1763 – French & Indian War Ends

February 16, 1923 – King Tut's Tomb Opened

February 19, 1912 – First Cracker Jack Prize

February 20, 1962 – John Glenn, 1st American to Orbit the Earth

February 23, 1896 – Tootsie Roll

February 23, 1945 – U.S. Marines raise American flag in Iwo Jima

February 28, 1692 – Salem Witch hunt begins

February 28, 1983 – Final episode of M.A.S.H. is aired

March 2, 1962 – Wilt Chamberlin scores 100 points against the Knicks

March 5, 1770 – Boston Massacre

March 6, 1836 – Fall of the Alamo

March 7, 1933 – Monopoly Invented (an hour later, little sisters begin to cheat as "banker")

March 8, 1971 – Joe Frazier beat Muhammad Ali in NY becoming Heavy Weight Champion

March 10, 1876 – First telephone call

March 11, 1818 – Frankenstein published

March 15, 44 B.C. – Cesar Assassinated

March 15, 1917 – Prohibition Begins

March 17 – St. Patrick's Day

March 28, 1881 – Barnum joins Bailey creating the Barnum & Bailey Circus

March 28, 1979 – 3 Mile Island Nuclear Power Plant Explosion

March 29, 1990 – First Warning Label on records

March 31, 1889 – Eiffel Tower

April 6, 1930 – Twinkies Invented

April 17, 1861 – Virginia secedes from the Union

April 15, 1450 – Battle of Formigny

April 19, 1897 – First Boston Marathon

April 25, 1901 – First U.S. License Plate

April 30, 1803 – Louisiana Purchase

May 1, 1931 – Empire State Building

May (The First Saturday In May) – Kentucky Derby

May 6, 1861 – Arkansas secedes from the Union

May 7, 1915 – Lusitania Sinks

May 8, 1945 – V.E. Day

May 12, 1847 – Odometer invented

May 14, 1804 – Lewis & Clark set out

May 14, 1998 – Last episode of *Seinfeld* is aired

May 16, 1929 – First Academy Awards

May 20, 1861 – North Carolina secedes from the Union

May 21, 1927 – Lindbergh lands I Paris

May 23, 1934 – Bonnie & Clyde get wacked by law enforcement officers

May 25,1977 – Star Wars released

May 27, 1937 – Golden Gate Bridge Opens

May 29, 1953 – Mt. Everest scaled for very first time by Sir Edmund Hillary

June 2, 1865 – War Between the States ends

June 4, 1917 – First Pulitzer Prizes

June 6, 1944 – D-Day

June 8, 1861 – Tennessee secedes from the Union

June 9, 1934 – Donald Duck Debut

June 12, 1880 – John Lee Richmond pitches baseball's first perfect game

June 16, 1884 – First Roller-Coaster

June 17, 1215 – King John signs the Magna Carta

June 18, 1815 – Napoleon at Waterloo

June 22, 1944 – G.I. Bill of Rights signed

June 23, 1860 – U.S. Secret Service in created

June 24, 1947 – First flying saucer report

June 28, 1919 – WWI ends

June 30, 1953 – First Corvette

July 3, 1886 – 1st auto test drive

July 5, 1946 – Bikini introduced

July 7, 1802 – 1st comic book printed

July 9, 1893 – First Open Heart Surgery

July 11, 1804 – Alexander Hamilton loses duel to Aaron Burr

July 17, 1955 – Disney Land opens

July 20, 1969 – 1st man on the moon

July 25, 1978 – 1st test tube baby born

July 26, 1908 – FBI founded

July 27, 1940 – Bugs Bunny debuts in Warner Brothers' *A Wild Hare*

July 29, 1958 – NASA founded

August 4, 1693 – Champagne is invented by Dom Perignon (I'll drink to that!)

August 4, 1790 – U.S. Coast Guard created

August 7, 1782 – The Order of the Purple Heart is created by George Washington.

August 9, 1930 – Betty Boop debuts in *Dirty Dishes*

August 10, 1846 – Smithsonian Created

August 11, 1909 – First SOS signal radioed

August 14, 1943 – VJ Day

August 15, 1057 – Macbeth is slain

August 15, 1969 – Woodstock begins

August 16, 1896 – Klondike gold discovered

August 18, 1872 – First Mail-Order Catalogue

August 19 – National Aviation Day

August 29, 1966 – Last Beatles concert

September 1, 1752 – Liberty Bell comes to Philadelphia

September 3, 1783 – End of American Revolution

September 6, 1620 – Mayflower set sail

September 7, 1813 – U.S. nicknamed Uncle Sam

September 8, 1966 – Star Trek premiers on television

September 13, 1788 – New York City becomes capitol of the United States

September 17, 1787 – U.S. Constitution signed

September 18, 1851 – 1st issue of the New York Times

September 24, 1968 – 60 Minutes debuts

September 25, 1789 – U.S. Bill of Rights adopted

September 29, 1899 – VFW established

October 1, 1903 – First World Series

October 2, 1950 – Peanuts cartoon debuts

October 9 – Leif Erikson Day

October 14, 1947 – Sound Barrier Broken

October 18, 1767 – Mason-Dixon Line established

October 22, 1962 – Cuban Missile Crisis

October 26, 1881 – Gun Fight at the OK Coral

October 27, 1904 – New York City Subway Opens

October 28, 1886 – Statue of Liberty dedicated

October 29, 1929 – Stock Market Crash, Great Depression Begins

October 31 – Boo!

November, 1638 – 1st J. Sitton arrives in New World sometime this month

November 3, 1956 – Wizard of Oz Television debut

November 4, 1841 – 1st wagon train reached California

November 9, 1989 – Berlin Wall comes down

November 10, 1775 – United States Marine Corps created

November 12, 1946 – 1st drive through bank (1st person through forgets to fill out forms, 2nd person annoyed)

November 13, 1940 – First Jeep

November 18, 1928 - Walt Disney's *Steamboat Willie* premieres introducing Mickey Mouse

November 21, 1620 – Mayflower lands

November 26, 1942 – Casablanca Released

November 28, 1895 – 1st U.S. auto race

December 3, 1967 – First Human Heart Transplant

*December 5, 1933 – Eighteenth Amendment Repealed

December 10, 1901 – 1st Nobel Prizes

December 14, 1947 – NASCAR founded

December 15, 1891 – Basketball invented

December 16, 1773 – Boston Tea Party

December 17, 1903 – 1st Wright Brothers Flight

December 19, 1972 – Apollo 17, last lunar landing

December 20, 1860 – South Carolina secedes from the Union

December 23, 1912 – Keystone Cops

December 27, 1904 – Peter Pan opens on stage

---

* It you don't know what the 18th Amendment was, you are probably not old enough for an "Adult Beverage".

APPENDIX – HAZARD LIGHTS USE

Alright, so if you have taken the time to read the essay and found yourself here let me explain. Below if a list of every state law and those of Canada when it comes to the use to hazard lights. I have provided a brief explanation and also the web site so you can view it your self.

United States

Alabama - <http://drivinglaws.aaa.com/us-motor-laws/alabama/hazard-light-use-57/> Alabama
<http://drivinglaws.aaa.com/category/us-motor-laws/alabama/>
The use of hazard lights is permitted unless otherwise posted.

Alaska - <http://drivinglaws.aaa.com/us-motor-laws/alaska/hazard-light-use-3/> Alaska
<http://drivinglaws.aaa.com/category/us-motor-laws/alaska/>
The use of hazard lights is not permitted.

Arizona - <http://drivinglaws.aaa.com/us-motor-laws/arizona/hazard-light-use-4/> Arizona
<http://drivinglaws.aaa.com/category/us-motor-laws/arizona/>
Hazard light use is not permitted except in an emergency situation.

Arkansas - <http://drivinglaws.aaa.com/us-motor-laws/arkansas/hazard-light-use-14/> Arkansas
<http://drivinglaws.aaa.com/category/us-motor-laws/arkansas/>
Hazard light usage is not permitted except to indicate a traffic hazard.

California - <http://drivinglaws.aaa.com/us-motor-laws/california/hazard-light-use-13/> <http://drivinglaws.aaa.com/category/us-motor-laws/california/>
Hazard light use is not permitted except to indicate a traffic hazard.

Colorado - <http://drivinglaws.aaa.com/us-motor-laws/colorado/hazard-light-use-12/> Colorado
<http://drivinglaws.aaa.com/category/us-motor-laws/colorado/>
Hazard light use is not permitted except if the vehicle speed is 25 mph or less.

Connecticut - <http://drivinglaws.aaa.com/us-motor-laws/connecticut/hazard-light-use-8/>
<http://drivinglaws.aaa.com/category/us-motor-laws/connecticut/>
Hazard light use is permitted unless otherwise posted.

Delaware - <http://drivinglaws.aaa.com/us-motor-laws/delaware/hazard-light-use-11/> Delaware
<http://drivinglaws.aaa.com/category/us-motor-laws/delaware/>
Hazard light use is not permitted except to indicate a traffic hazard.

D.C. - <http://drivinglaws.aaa.com/us-motor-laws/district-of-columbia/hazard-light-use-10/> District of Columbia <http://drivinglaws.aaa.com/category/us-motor-laws/district-of-columbia/>
Hazard light use is permitted.

Florida - <http://drivinglaws.aaa.com/us-motor-laws/florida/hazard-light-use-9/> Florida
<http://drivinglaws.aaa.com/category/us-motor-laws/florida/>
The use of hazard lights is not permitted

Georgia - <http://drivinglaws.aaa.com/us-motor-laws/georgia/hazard-light-use-55/> Georgia
<http://drivinglaws.aaa.com/category/us-motor-laws/georgia/>
The use of hazard lights is permitted.

Hawaii - <http://drivinglaws.aaa.com/us-motor-laws/hawaii/hazard-light-use-16/> Hawaii
<http://drivinglaws.aaa.com/category/us-motor-laws/hawaii/>
Hazard light use is not permitted.

Idaho - <http://drivinglaws.aaa.com/us-motor-laws/idaho/hazard-light-use-17/> Idaho
<http://drivinglaws.aaa.com/category/us-motor-laws/idaho/>
Hazard light use is not permitted except to indicate the presence of a vehicular traffic hazard
requiring unusual care in approaching, overtaking or passing.

Illinois - <http://drivinglaws.aaa.com/us-motor-laws/illinois/hazard-light-use-15/> Illinois
<http://drivinglaws.aaa.com/category/us-motor-laws/illinois/>
The use of hazard lights is not permitted.

Indiana - <http://drivinglaws.aaa.com/us-motor-laws/indiana/hazard-light-use-18/> Indiana
<http://drivinglaws.aaa.com/category/us-motor-laws/indiana/>
Hazard light use is not permitted except in emergency situations.

Iowa - <http://drivinglaws.aaa.com/us-motor-laws/iowa/hazard-light-use-20/> Iowa
<http://drivinglaws.aaa.com/category/us-motor-laws/iowa/>
The use of hazard lights are not permitted except to indicate a traffic hazard.

Kansas - <http://drivinglaws.aaa.com/us-motor-laws/kansas/hazard-light-use-21/> Kansas
<http://drivinglaws.aaa.com/category/us-motor-laws/kansas/>
Hazard light use is not permitted.

Kentucky - <http://drivinglaws.aaa.com/us-motor-laws/kentucky/hazard-light-use-22/>
<http://drivinglaws.aaa.com/category/us-motor-laws/kentucky/>
Hazard light use is permitted.

Louisiana - <http://drivinglaws.aaa.com/us-motor-laws/louisiana/hazard-light-use-23/>
<http://drivinglaws.aaa.com/category/us-motor-laws/louisiana/>
Hazard light use is not permitted.

Maine - <http://drivinglaws.aaa.com/us-motor-laws/maine/hazard-light-use-24/> Maine
<http://drivinglaws.aaa.com/category/us-motor-laws/maine/>
Hazard light use is not permitted, unless to indicate a traffic hazard.

Maryland <http://drivinglaws.aaa.com/us-motor-laws/maryland/hazard-light-use-25/> Maryland
<http://drivinglaws.aaa.com/category/us-motor-laws/maryland/>
Hazard light use is not permitted except in emergency situations.

Massachusetts-<http://drivinglaws.aaa.com/us-motor-laws/massachusetts/hazard-light-use-26/>
<http://drivinglaws.aaa.com/category/us-motor-laws/massachusetts/>
Hazard light use is not permitted.

Michigan - <http://drivinglaws.aaa.com/us-motor-laws/michigan/hazard-light-use-27/> Michigan
<http://drivinglaws.aaa.com/category/us-motor-laws/michigan/>
Hazard light use is permitted.

Minnesota-<http://drivinglaws.aaa.com/us-motor-laws/minnesota/hazard-light-use-28/>
<http://drivinglaws.aaa.com/category/us-motor-laws/minnesota/>
Hazard lights are not permitted except to indicate a traffic hazard.

Mississippi - <http://drivinglaws.aaa.com/us-motor-laws/mississippi/hazard-light-use-29/>
<http://drivinglaws.aaa.com/category/us-motor-laws/mississippi/>
Hazard light usage is permitted.

Missouri - <http://drivinglaws.aaa.com/us-motor-laws/missouri/hazard-light-use-30/> Missouri
<http://drivinglaws.aaa.com/category/us-motor-laws/missouri/>
Hazard light usage is permitted.

Montana - <http://drivinglaws.aaa.com/us-motor-laws/montana/hazard-light-use-31/> Montana
<http://drivinglaws.aaa.com/category/us-motor-laws/montana/>
Hazard lights are not permitted except to indicate a traffic hazard.

Nebraska - <http://drivinglaws.aaa.com/us-motor-laws/nebraska/hazard-light-use-32/> Nebraska
<http://drivinglaws.aaa.com/category/us-motor-laws/nebraska/>
Hazard light use is permitted.

Nevada - <http://drivinglaws.aaa.com/us-motor-laws/nevada/hazard-light-use-33/> Nevada
<http://drivinglaws.aaa.com/category/us-motor-laws/nevada/>
Hazard light usage is not permitted.

New Hampashire - <http://drivinglaws.aaa.com/us-motor-laws/new-hampshire/hazard-light-use-48/>
<http://drivinglaws.aaa.com/category/us-motor-laws/new-hampshire/>
Hazard light use is permitted.

New Jersey - <http://drivinglaws.aaa.com/us-motor-laws/new-jersey/hazard-light-use-56/>
<http://drivinglaws.aaa.com/category/us-motor-laws/new-jersey/>
The use of hazard lights is not permitted.

New Mexico - <http://drivinglaws.aaa.com/us-motor-laws/new-mexico/hazard-light-use-49/>
<http://drivinglaws.aaa.com/category/us-motor-laws/new-mexico/>
Hazard light use is not permitted.

New York - <http://drivinglaws.aaa.com/us-motor-laws/new-york/hazard-light-use-50/>
<http://drivinglaws.aaa.com/category/us-motor-laws/new-york/>
Hazard light use is permitted unless otherwise posted.

North Carolina - <http://drivinglaws.aaa.com/us-motor-laws/north-carolina/hazard-light-use-51/>
<http://drivinglaws.aaa.com/category/us-motor-laws/north-carolina/>
Hazard light use is permitted unless otherwise posted.

North Dakota - <http://drivinglaws.aaa.com/us-motor-laws/north-dakota/hazard-light-use-52/>
<http://drivinglaws.aaa.com/category/us-motor-laws/north-dakota/>
Hazard light use is permitted unless otherwise posted.

Ohio - <http://drivinglaws.aaa.com/us-motor-laws/ohio/hazard-light-use-53/> Ohio
<http://drivinglaws.aaa.com/category/us-motor-laws/ohio/>
Hazard light use is not permitted, except when a hazardous condition is present.

Oklahoma-<http://drivinglaws.aaa.com/us-motor-laws/oklahoma/hazard-light-use-54/>
<http://drivinglaws.aaa.com/category/us-motor-laws/oklahoma/>
Hazard light use is not permitted except in emergency situations and to indicate a traffic hazard.

Oregon - <http://drivinglaws.aaa.com/us-motor-laws/oregon/hazard-light-use-34/> Oregon
<http://drivinglaws.aaa.com/category/us-motor-laws/oregon/>
Hazard light use is permitted unless otherwise posted.

Pennsylvania - <http://drivinglaws.aaa.com/us-motor-laws/pennsylvania/hazard-light-use-35/>
<http://drivinglaws.aaa.com/category/us-motor-laws/pennsylvania/>
Hazard lights are permitted.

Rhode Island - <http://drivinglaws.aaa.com/us-motor-laws/rhode-island/hazard-light-use-36/>
<http://drivinglaws.aaa.com/category/us-motor-laws/rhode-island/>
Hazard light use is not permitted.

South Carolina - <http://drivinglaws.aaa.com/us-motor-laws/south-carolina/hazard-light-use-37/>
<http://drivinglaws.aaa.com/category/us-motor-laws/south-carolina/>
Hazard lights may be used for the purpose of warning the operators of other vehicles of the presence of a vehicular traffic hazard requiring the exercise of unusual care in approaching, overtaking or passing.

South Dakota - <http://drivinglaws.aaa.com/us-motor-laws/south-dakota/hazard-light-use-38/>
<http://drivinglaws.aaa.com/category/us-motor-laws/south-dakota/>
Hazard light use is permitted.

Tennessee-<http://drivinglaws.aaa.com/us-motor-laws/tennessee/hazard-light-use-39/>
<http://drivinglaws.aaa.com/category/us-motor-laws/tennessee/>
Hazard light use is not permitted except in emergency situations.

Texas-<http://drivinglaws.aaa.com/us-motor-laws/texas/hazard-light-use-40/> Texas
<http://drivinglaws.aaa.com/category/us-motor-laws/texas/>
Hazard light use is permitted.

Utah - <http://drivinglaws.aaa.com/us-motor-laws/utah/hazard-light-use-41/> Utah
<http://drivinglaws.aaa.com/category/us-motor-laws/utah/>
Hazard light use is permitted.

Vermont - <http://drivinglaws.aaa.com/us-motor-laws/vermont/hazard-light-use-42/> Vermont
<http://drivinglaws.aaa.com/category/us-motor-laws/vermont/>
Hazard light use is permitted.

Virginia - <http://drivinglaws.aaa.com/us-motor-laws/virginia/hazard-light-use-43/> Virginia
<http://drivinglaws.aaa.com/category/us-motor-laws/virginia/>
Hazard light use is not permitted except for emergency vehicles, stopped or slowed vehicles to indicate a traffic hazard, when traveling as part of a funeral procession, or traveling slower than 30 mph.

Washington - <http://drivinglaws.aaa.com/us-motor-laws/washington/hazard-light-use-44/>
<http://drivinglaws.aaa.com/category/us-motor-laws/washington/>
Hazard light use is not permitted except to indicate a traffic hazard.

West Virginia - <http://drivinglaws.aaa.com/us-motor-laws/west-virginia/hazard-light-use-45/>
<http://drivinglaws.aaa.com/category/us-motor-laws/west-virginia/>
Hazard lights are not permitted except in emergency situations.

Wisconsin-<http://drivinglaws.aaa.com/us-motor-laws/wisconsin/hazard-light-use-46/>
<http://drivinglaws.aaa.com/category/us-motor-laws/wisconsin/>
Hazard lights are not permitted except to indicate a traffic hazard or when a hazardous condition is present.

Wyoming-<http://drivinglaws.aaa.com/us-motor-laws/wyoming/hazard-light-use-47/>
<http://drivinglaws.aaa.com/category/us-motor-laws/wyoming/>
Hazard light use is permitted.

Puerto Rico - <http://drivinglaws.aaa.com/us-motor-laws/puerto-rico/hazard-light-use-63/>
<http://drivinglaws.aaa.com/category/us-motor-laws/puerto-rico/>
Hazard light use is not permitted.

Canada

Hazard Light Use - for Canada go to <http://drivinglaws.aaa.com/laws/hazard-light-use/#quickjumpCanada>)

Alberta - <http://drivinglaws.aaa.com/canadian-motor-laws/alberta/hazard-light-use/> Alberta
<http://drivinglaws.aaa.com/category/canadian-motor-laws/alberta/>
The use of hazard lights is required by passenger vehicles that are stationary on a highway outside of an urban area at night or when the vehicle is not visible from 150 meters distance.

British Columbia - <http://drivinglaws.aaa.com/canadian-motor-laws/british-columbia/hazard-light-use-6/>
<http://drivinglaws.aaa.com/category/canadian-motor-laws/british-columbia/>
Hazard lights may be used when operating a slow-moving vehicle or when a vehicle is disabled on the highway.

Manitoba - <http://drivinglaws.aaa.com/canadian-motor-laws/manitoba/hazard-light-use-7/>
<http://drivinglaws.aaa.com/category/canadian-motor-laws/manitoba/>
Hazard lights may be used when a motor vehicle is coming to a stop or standing on a highway or traveling at a speed less than 40 kph when it is necessary to do so for safe operation; and when the vehicle is again put in motion or resumes a speed up to 40 kph.

New Brunswick - <http://drivinglaws.aaa.com/canadian-motor-laws/new-brunswick/hazard-light-use-19/>
<http://drivinglaws.aaa.com/category/canadian-motor-laws/new-brunswick/>
Hazard lights are permitted only when a vehicle is parked on the highway or any portion thereof due to an emergency or under circumstances beyond the control of the driver.

Newfoundland and Labrador - <http://drivinglaws.aaa.com/canadian-motor-laws/newfoundland-and-labrador/hazard-light-use-58/>
<http://drivinglaws.aaa.com/category/canadian-motor-laws/newfoundland-and-labrador/>
Hazard light use is permitted.

Northwest Territories - <http://drivinglaws.aaa.com/canadian-motor-laws/northwest-territories/hazard-light-use-59/>
<http://drivinglaws.aaa.com/category/canadian-motor-laws/northwest-territories/>
Hazard lights must be used when a vehicle is parked on a roadway under during the period from 1 hour after sunset to1 hour before sunrise or at any other time when conditions of poor visibility exist. A vehicle that is travelling at less than 40 km/h, owing to vehicle impairment, must have its hazard lights activated.

Nova Scotia - <http://drivinglaws.aaa.com/canadian-motor-laws/nova-scotia/hazard-light-use-60/>
<http://drivinglaws.aaa.com/category/canadian-motor-laws/nova-scotia/>
Hazard light use is permitted.

Nunavut - <http://drivinglaws.aaa.com/canadian-motor-laws/nunavut/hazard-light-use-2/>
<http://drivinglaws.aaa.com/category/canadian-motor-laws/nunavut/>
Hazard lights are required to be activated when a driver parks a vehicle on a roadway during the period from 1/2 hour after sunset to 1/2 hour before sunrise or at any other time when conditions of poor visibility exist; or when the vehicle is travelling at less than 40 km/h due to vehicle impairment.

Ontario - <http://drivinglaws.aaa.com/canadian-motor-laws/ontario/hazard-light-use-61/>
<http://drivinglaws.aaa.com/category/canadian-motor-laws/ontario/>
There are no restrictions on hazard light use.

Prince Edward Island - <http://drivinglaws.aaa.com/canadian-motor-laws/prince-edward-island/hazard-light-use-62/>
<http://drivinglaws.aaa.com/category/canadian-motor-laws/prince-edward-island/>
Hazard lights may not be used on a highway when a vehicle is moving.

Quebec - <http://drivinglaws.aaa.com/canadian-motor-laws/quebec/hazard-light-use-5/> Quebec
<http://drivinglaws.aaa.com/category/canadian-motor-laws/quebec/>
Hazard light use is permitted only for safety reasons.

Saskatchewan - <http://drivinglaws.aaa.com/canadian-motor-laws/saskatchewan/hazard-light-use-65/>
<http://drivinglaws.aaa.com/category/canadian-motor-laws/saskatchewan/>
Hazard lights may not be used unless a vehicle is coming to a stop or is standing on a highway, it is necessary to do so for the safe operation of the vehicle, or the vehicle presents a hazard to other vehicles on the highway.

Yukon - <http://drivinglaws.aaa.com/category/canadian-motor-laws/yukon/>
Hazard lights are permitted to indicate a hazard.

APPENDIX -
LIST OF IMPORTANT PHILOSOPHERS

John Locke

Believed all knowledge was gained through experience. His publication in 1689 of *An Essay Concerning Human Understanding* is one of the first defenses of EMPIRICISM.

Why He Is Important

John Locke had little use for the notion of the "Divine Rights of Kings". The Founding Fathers of the United States were deeply influenced by his philosophy, especially the notion of a "social contract".

He believed mankind had "certain inalienable rights", (Sound familiar?), and those rights are to be gained by working for them, not by the "nobles oblige" of the sitting liege or from a welfare state.

The system of capitalism is an economic expression of John Locke's principles.

He is also famous for his notion of a "social contract". Locke saw the contract as being between society and the government to protect the rights of the individual. Basically it is understood he felt that a citizen was not required to remain silent. If displeased, the citizen had the right to pack up and leave or to change whatever the grievance may be. The architects of the French and American Revolution picked up on this idea and extended it further.

Epicurus

He has been commonly misunderstood or mischaracterized as an advocate of the hedonistic rampant pursuit of pleasure. However, if you take all of his teachings/thoughts, (*I would say writings but very few complete works have survived), together, I have found him to be an advocate of seeking the absence of pain and suffering. He taught when we do not suffer pain, we are no longer in need of pleasure. Epicurus emphasized minimizing harm and maximizing happiness of oneself and others, "neither to harm or to be harmed". He argued displeasures in life do exist and must be avoided in order enter a state of perfect mental peace. Some other teachings included:

- It is impossible to live a pleasant life without living wisely and well and justly.
- It is impossible to live wisely and justly without living a pleasant life.

I love the duality and linkage of those two statements; you need to do one thing but cannot do one without the other. So much of life is exactly that. For instance, I would not be living a happy life without my lovely wife. (That ought to score me some points at home.)

To Epicurus or in the Epicurean view:

- wisely would be avoidance of pain, danger, disease
- well would be proper diet and physical exertion
- Justly would be not to harm others because you do not want to be harmed, (basically the Golden Rule).

Epicurus regularly admitted women and slaves into his school showing his egalitarian views which come through in his doctrines.

---

* Surviving <u>complete</u> works are three letters found in book ten of *Lives of Eminent Philosophers*, a group of quotes, and the *Vatican Sayings* preserved in the Vatican Library.

This is quite different from the 'mardi gra –ish' lifestyle often associated with him. He was actually seeking and teaching the pursuit of *ataraxia*. (Defined in Webster's Dictionary as – peace of mind: TRANQUILLITY)

- It should be noted, to Epicurus, pleasure and pain were both physical and mental.

Another departure from the hedonistic view of him held by many, was Epicurus warned against overindulgence as it often leads to pain. This seems to me to be in line with the teaching of the Catholic Church. For instance, the Church does not ban the consumption of alcohol, but it does warn against over consumption.

Epicurus was not an atheist and many arguments against the existence of gods were wrongly attributed to him by early Christians and their perspectives. He participated in the activities of traditional Greek religion, but taught you should avoid holding false opinions about the gods. He did not deny the existence, he simply stated the gods, (whatever they may be), do not concern themselves with humans and therefore would not seek to punish the bad or reward the good.

Why He Is Important

Elements of his philosophy have found meaning and have often resurfaced throughout Western History. The ethic of reciprocity influenced democratic thinkers of the French Revolution.

He had great influence on John Locke.

His egalitarianism views influenced the American freedom movement and can be seen in the Declaration of Independence. (Thomas Jefferson considered himself an Epicurean.)

Zeno of Citium

Zeno founded the philosophical school of Stoicism in the Hellenistic period. Stoicism is based upon the idea that anything which causes us to suffer in life is actually a false judgment and people should have absolute control over their emotions, always. Envy, rage, elation, depression, impassioned sexual attachments, or passionate love of anything; these are all flaws in a person's reason and thus we are only emotionally weak when we allow ourselves to be. Put another way, the world is what you make of it.

Zeno and those who followed the Stoicism, "Stoics", did not consider their philosophy as an interesting pastime or even a particular body of knowledge, but as a way of life. Much like those, who now, follow the teachings of Catholicism or Judaism, which should be a way a life, not just a title you give yourself. Put another way, they practiced what they preached. This element helps to explain why Stoicism was eventually eclipsed by Christianity, in the same way the Samurai were easy converts to Christianity in feudal Japan.

Why He Is Important

Just think of our common era phrase, "Stoic Calm".

Avicenna

Ibn Sina is often known by his Latin name of Avicenna, was an Islamic philosopher and physician who authored commentaries to the work of Aristotle as well as Canons of Medicine; which became indispensable in western universities and other encyclopedic works. He became interested in the relationship between the beign and its essence and between the possible and the necessary. God is the necessary being where essence and existence merge. His thoughts provoqued interesting debates during the Middle Ages and the Renaissance.

Avicenna (Ibn Sina) two most important works are The Book of Healing and The Canon of Medicine. The first is a scientific encyclopedia covering logic, natural sciences, psychology, geometry, astronomy, arithmetic and music. The second is the most famous single book in the history of medicine.

Avicenna (Ibn Sina) wrote about four-hundred-fifty works, which around two-hundred-forty have survived. Of the surviving works, about half are on philosophy while the others are devoted to medicine; the two fields in which he contributed most. He also wrote on psychology, geology, mathematics, astronomy, and logic. According to many, his most important work as far as mathematics is concerned is his immense encyclopedic work, the *The Book of* Healing (Kitab al-Shifa'). One of the four parts of this work is devoted to mathematics and Avicenna includes astronomy and music as branches of mathematics within the encyclopaedia. In fact he divided mathematics into four branches, geometry, astronomy, arithmetic, and music, and he then subdivided each of these topics. Geometry he subdivided into geodesy, statics, kinematics, hydrostatics, and optics; astronomy he subdivided into astronomical and geographical tables, and the calendar; arithmetic he subdivided into algebra, and Indian addition and subtraction; music he subdivided into musical instruments.

In the medieval Islamic world, due to Avicenna's successful reconciliation between Aristotelianism and Neoplatonism along with

Kalam, Avicenna's thought system Avicennism eventually became the leading school of Islamic philosophy by the 12th century, with Avicenna becoming a central authority on philosophy.

Avicennism was also influential in medieval Europe, particular his doctrines on the nature of the soul and his existence-essence distinction, along with the debates and censure that they raised in scholastic Europe. This was particularly the case in Paris, where Avicennism was later proscribed in 1210. Nevertheless, his psychology and theory of knowledge influenced William of Auvergne, Bishop of Paris and Albertus Magnus, while his metaphysics had an impact on the thought of Thomas Aquinas.

Why He Is Important

As Avicenna (Ibn Sina) considered music as one of the branches of mathematics and I like both music and certain aspects of math. His work on this topic was mainly on tonic intervals, rhythmic patterns, and musical instruments.

Thomas Aquinas

Aquinas will most likely be remembered as the one who supposedly proved the existence of God by arguing the Universe had to have been created by something, since everything in existence has a beginning and an end. This is referred to as the "First Cause" argument, and philosophers after Aquinas have spent their time attempting to prove or disprove this argument. Aquinas actually based his argument on Aristotle's notion of "one who moves while not moving" or "the unmoved mover".

Aquinas founded everything he presented firmly in Christianity. For this reason he is not usually mentioned is discussions about important philosophers. Even among many Christian theologians Aquinas is not considered independently authoritative since he derived all of his ethical teachings from the Bible.

However, if you consider what 'his job' was, and how he taught the people, lay persons, his ability to relate and explain is as extraordinary as any other philosopher I listed. He was able to explain ethics without abstract philosophy. Aquinas expounded upon Plato's "cardinal virtues" and was able to reach the masses with a simple four-part instruction: Justice – Courage – Prudence – Temperance. (I wonder if he reached the masses in Mass.)

Why He Is Important

Aquinas made five famous arguments for the existence of God which are to this day still discussed passionately on both sides; theist and atheist.

Of those five, which he intended to define the nature of God, on is called, "The Unity of God", which states, God is not divisible, but has essence and existence. Those two qualities cannot be separated. Therefore, if you are able to express something as possessing two or more qualities and cannot separate the qualities, then the statement itself proves there is a God.

Aquinas' example is the statement, "God exists.", in which the statement subject and predicate are identical.

Confucius

He was a traveling philosopher who lived in a time of chaos and corruption in ancient China and his philosophy stressed the ethical importance in interpersonal and political relations and family values, emphasizing a deep respect for parents and older siblings as the most basic form of promoting the interests of others before yourself. In other words, The Golden Rule. This is also evident in his quote, "What you do not wish for yourself do not do to others;".

According to tradition, Confucius was an educator, (he founded the "Ru" School of Chinese thought.), thinker, and political figure.

Some maintain that Confucius contradicts himself with regards to religion. In my opinion, this is only true when his teachings are viewed from a Western point view. When doing so, one can see both Catholic and Protestant beliefs. He believed that, *"people live their lives within parameters firmly established by Heaven – which, often, for him means both a purposeful Supreme Being as well as 'nature' and its fixed cycles and patterns-..." (Protestant). He argues that "men are responsible for their actions..."(Catholic). Men are especially responsible for their treatment of others. We can do little or nothing to alter our fated span of existence (Protestant) but we determine what we accomplish and what we are remembered for (Catholic).

Confucius has been compared to having as must influence on Chinese culture and history as Socrates had in Western Culture. To me, it is amazing how much, when broken down, the beliefs of the West and the East have in common. This could be used to argue we are all human and should be able to get along without conflict. Of course being "human", as I wrote earlier, also means being selfish, which leads to conflict.

Why He Is Important

His view of the political institutions of his day troubled him. Confucius believed that when a person possessed a title and participated in the various duties signified by that title, then they should live up to the meaning of that title. He saw and believed the political institutions had completely broken down because those in power had stopped governing in a way that benefitted the people but wielded power in a way which benefitted themselves. Does this sound familiar to you?

*Stanford Encyclopedia of Philosophy

Rene' Descartes

He was a French philosopher, writer and mathematician whom I have quoted often in different essays. At times his bibliography reads like an action spy novel*. Noted for both this philosophical and mathematical writings he was a key figure in the Scientific Revolution and was often described as an example of a genius.

Descartes served in the military, was educated in mathematics, physics, and even studied law. He published both philosophy and mathematical works throughout his life and was dominating in each field.

Why He Is Important:

He contributed to mathematics (combining geometry and algebra) and philosophical thought.

He stated: "Cogito ergo sum". I think therefore I am.

---

* There is a theory he was actually killed by a Catholic Priest and did not die of pneumonia in his bed.

Paul of Tarsus

Although much written about him may seem more theological than philosophical, Paul of Tarsus had a brilliant mind, commanding knowledge of philosophy and religion, and could debate with the most educate d scholars of the day. He was also a former Pharisee, tax collector, and Christian "hunter". The exact number of Christian executions he was responsible for is unknown.

After his conversion to Christianity, Paul is often credited with bringing the faith to the Gentiles and helping to make Christianity a universal religion.

Why he is important

Simply put, if Paul was able to repent for his sins and ask for God's forgiveness, then it should be much easier for you and I.

Plato

Was Socrates most famous disciple and used his dialectical style of debate: the pursuit of truth through questions.

Founded the Academy often described as the first European University

His writings were in dialog form; written in the content of a conversation or debate involving two or more persons.

His impact of Jewish thought is apparent in the work of the 1st century

He was among other things a political philosopher

Why He Is Important

All of Plato's writings and works are in some way meant to leave further work for the readers. In other words, many of the philosophers who followed used Plato's works as a starting point or springboard for their own.

Aristotle

Realizing of course listing him is almost cheating considering both he and Plato share the distinction of being the most famous philosophers, I am still going to do it. Aristotle, along with others on my 'list' contributed much in the way we live today.

Writing Aristotle studied under Plato almost seems like a waste of time; we all know that, or at least everyone knows one studied under the other. He studied and taught at Plato's Academy for approximately twenty years. After the death of Plato, Aristotle left, traveled, settled in one place and then another. That other place was Macedonian capital city, Pella. There he landed what many would call a 'pretty sweet gig.' He became the tutor of the King's young son. The boy, Alexander, is who we now refer to as Alexander the Great. Okay, history lesson over. Why is he on my 'list'?

Why He Is Important

Aristotle wrote a dictionary of philosophic terms. He wrote a summary of the doctrine of Pythagoras. (All those who despised Algebra and Calculus may now think of him differently. That is assuming you think of him at all.)

APPENDIX – CLICHÉS

- Absence makes the heart grow fonder
- Add insult to injury
- Age before beauty
- Agonizing reappraisal
- Agree to disagree
- Albatross around one's neck
- All in a day's work
- All in the same boat
- All over but the crying
- All over but the shouting
- All things being equal
- All things to all men
- All work and no play
- Apple of one's eye
- Armed to the teeth
- Arms of Morpheus
- As luck would have it
- At a loss for words
- At first blush
- At sixes and sevens
- Axe to grind

- Bag and baggage
- Bark up the wrong tree
- Bated breath
- Bathed in tears

- Beard the lion in his den
- Beat a dead horse
- Beat a hasty retreat
- Beat around the bush
- Beg to disagree
- Beggar description
- Bend over backward
- Best foot forward
- Best laid plans
- Best of all possible worlds
- Better late than never
- Between the devil and the deep blue sea
- Beyond the call of duty
- Beyond the pale
- Bigger than all outdoors
- Bigger than life
- Bite of more than one can chew
- Bite the bullet
- Blushing bride
- Blush of shame
- Boggle the mind
- Bolt from the blue
- Bone of contention
- Born with a silver spoon
- Bosom of the family
- Brave the elements
- Breathe a sigh of relief
- Bright and early
- Bright as a button
- Bright-eyed and bushy-tailed
- Bright future
- Bring home the bacon
- Brown as a berry
- Budding genius

- Bull in a china shop
- Burn the midnight oil
- Busy as a bee
- Butter wouldn't melt in one's mouth
- By leaps and bounds
- By the same token

- Calm before the storm
- Can't see the forest for the trees
- Carry a chip on one's shoulder
- Carry the coals to Newcastle
- Case in point
- Caught on the horns of a dilemma
- Caught red handed
- Chip off the old block
- Clear as mud
- Coin a phrase
- Cold as ice
- Conspicuous by ones absence
- Cool as a cumber
- Cross the Rubicon
- Crying need
- Cut a long story short
- Cut off one's nose to spite one's face
- Cynosure of all eyes

- Daily repast
- Dead as a doornail
- Defend to the death one's right to...
- Depths of despair
- Depths of one's desire
- Diamond in the rough

- Die in Harness
- Die is cast
- Distaff side
- Do it up brown
- Do one's thing
- Dog in the manger
- Doom is sealed (Fate)
- Doomed to disappointment
- Down in the dumps
- Down in the mouth
- Down the hatch
- Down's one's alley
- Draw the line
- Drown one's sorrows
- Drunk as a lord/skunk
- Dull thud

- Early bird gets the worm
- Early to bed, early to rise
- Ear to the ground
- Easier said than done
- Eat one's hat/words
- Epoch making
- Eternal reward
- Eyes of the world

- Face the music
- (the) Fair sex
- Fall on deaf ears
- Far be it for me
- (a) Far cry
- Fast and loose

- Fate is sealed
- Fate worse than death
- Fat's in the fire
- Feather in one's cap
- Feel one's oats
- Festive board
- Few and far between
- Few well-chosen words
- Fiddle while Rome burns
- Fight like a tiger
- Fill the bill
- Filthy lucre
- Fine and dandy
- First and foremost
- Fit as a fiddle
- Flash in the pan
- Flat as a flounder
- Flat as a pancake
- Flesh and blood
- Fly off the handle
- Fond farewell
- Food for thought
- Fools rush in
- Foot in one's mouth
- Foot the bill
- Foregone conclusion
- Forewarned is forearmed
- Free as a bird (the air)
- Fresh as a daisy

- Generous to a fault
- Gentle as a lamb
- Get down to brass tacks

- Get one's dander up
- Get one's back up
- (a) Good time was had by all
- Goose that laid the golden egg
- Grain of salt
- Grand and glorious
- Graphic account
- Green-eyed monster
- Grin like a Cheshire cat
- Grind to a halt

- Hail fellow well met
- Hale and hearty
- Hand that rocks the cradle
- Handsome is as handsome does
- Handwriting on the wall
- Hapless victim
- Happy as a lark
- Happy pair
- Hard row to hoe
- Haughty stare
- Haul over the coals (Rake)
- Have a foot in the door
- Have a leg up
- Head over heals
- Heart of gold
- Heave a sigh of relief
- Hew to the line
- High and dry
- High as a kite
- High on the hog
- Hit the nail on the head
- Hit the spot

- Hook, line, and sinker
- Hook or crook
- Hot as a firecracker (pistol)
- Hue and cry
- Hungry as a bear (lion)

- If (the) truth be told
- In full swing
- In no uncertain terms
- In on the ground floor
- In seventh heaven
- Inspiring sight
- In the final analysis
- In the limelight
- In the long run
- In the nick of time
- In this day and age
- Iron out a difficulty
- Irons in the fire
- Irony of fate
- Irreparable damage
- It goes without saying
- It is interesting to note
- It never rains but it pours
- It's an ill wind
- It's six of one and a half a dozen of the other
- It stands to reason
- It takes all kinds to make a world
- It takes two to tango

- Jig is up
- Jump down my (your) throat

- Jump the gun
- Just deserts
- Just the tip of the iceberg

- Keep a low profile
- Keep a stiff upper lip
- Keeps his cards close to his chest
- Knee-high to a grasshopper
- Knock into a cocked hat
- Knock on wood
- Knocked it out of the park

- Labor of love
- Larger than life
- Last but not least
- Last straw
- Law unto one's self
- Lead to the altar
- Lean and hungry look
- Lean over backward
- Leave in the lurch
- Leave no stone unturned
- Left-handed compliment
- Lend a helping hand
- Let one's hair down
- Let the cat out of the bag
- Let well enough alone
- Lick into shape
- Lid of secrecy
- Like a house afire
- Like a new born babe
- Limp as a dish rag

- Lock, stock, and barrel
- Long arm of the law
- Look a gift horse in the mouth

- Make a hasty retreat
- Make heads or tails of
- Make the grade
- Make waves
- Meet one's Waterloo
- Melts in one's mouth
- (a) Mexican standoff
- More sinned against than sinning

- Never at a loss for words
- Never say die
- No pain, no gain
- No skin off my nose
- No strings attached

- Old as dirt
- On the same page
- Out of the woods

- Paint yourself into a corner
- Pull the wool over your eyes
- Put two and two together
- Put it on the back burner
- Put that in your pipe and smoke it

- Red-letter day
- Right up your alley
- Rock the boat
- Rome wasn't built in a day

- See the light
- Show the white feather

- Take one for the team
- Time flies when you are having fun
- Time heals all wounds
- Time is money
- That's what she said
- Through thick and thin
- Too many chiefs, not enough Indians
- Too rich for my blood
- Two heads are better than one

- Ugly as sin
- Up a creek without a paddle
- Until the cows come home
- Useless as tits on a boar hog

- Value of tears
- Variety is the spice of life

- Wake up and smell the roses
- Walking on eggshells
- (a) Watched pot never boils

- What's good for the goose is good for the gander
- When it rains, it pours
- Without further ado

- Yank your chain
- You can lead a horse to water. But you can't make him drink
- You can never go home again
- You can say that again
- You can't make a silk purse out of a sow's ear
- You must crawl before you can walk

- Zigged when he should have zagged
- Zip your lip

APPENDIX – WEB SITES

www.treasurydirect.gov/NP/debt/current

"To Find out the total public debt outstanding on a specific day or days, simply select a single date or date range and click on the 'Find History' button. The debt held by the public versus intragovernmental holdings data is available.

www.refdesk.com

This site is my home page. Refdesk is a free and family friendly web site that indexes and reviews quality, credible, and current web-based reference resources. Such as: Newspapers US and Worldwide, Dictionaries, Site of the Day Archive, Weather Resources, even Crosswords.

www.khanacademy.org

Khan Academy. "With a library of over 3,000 videos covering everything from arithmetic to physics, finance, and history and hundreds of skills to practice, we're on a mission to help you learn what you want, when you want, at your own pace."

www.onelook.com

OneLook Dictionary Search. The website is a search engine for words and phrases.

www.statelocalgov.net

State and Local Government on the Net. "The State and Local Government Internet Directory provides convenient one-stop access to the websites of thousands of state agencies and city and county governments. Use the drop-down menu to access."

https://archive.org/details/feature_films

Internet Archives: FREE MOVIES. "Feature Films, shorts, silent films and trailers are available for viewing and downloading. Enjoy! View a list of all the Feature Films sorted by popularity."

https://www.ixquick.com

ixquick. "Ixquick search provides search results from over the ten best search engines in full privacy. Search anonymously with ixquick search engine!" "TAKE A DEEP BREATH. YOU'RE SAFE HERE."

www.bbc.co.uk/religion/religious

BBC: Guide to World Religions. "Guides to world religions and beliefs Includes Atheism, Christianity, Islam, Paganism, Jainism, Zoroastrain, and many more."

www.TuneIn.com

"The Web has all sorts of sites for audio. TuneIn is a comprehensive web site which is very simple to use for listening to 50,000 sources of audio programs in one place. Sports, music, news, local, etc… It also has an app for the iPhone, iPad, Andriod and other devices."

www.songza.com

Create audio playlists

www.devour.com

Some say it is better than YouTube

www.AtariArcade.com

Play classic Atari Video Games

www.coursera.com

College courses for free.

www.codeacademy.com

Learn to write code. Learn to build a personal website.

Made in the USA
Lexington, KY
14 November 2014